T0352454

MILITARY MONEY GUIDE

P.J. Budahn

STACKPOLE
BOOKS

Copyright © 1996 by Stackpole Books

Published by
STACKPOLE BOOKS
5067 Ritter Road
Mechanicsburg, PA 17055

This book is not an official publication of the Department of Defense, nor does its publication in any way imply its endorsement by this agency.

Cover design by Tina M. Hill

Printed in the United States of America

First Edition

10 9 8 7 6 5 4 3 2 1

Library of Congress Cataloging-in-Publication Data

Budahn, P. J. (Philip J.), 1949–
   Military money guide / P.J. Budahn. — 1st ed.
      p.   cm.
   Includes index.
   ISBN 0-8117-2557-X (alk. paper)
      1. United States—Armed Forces—Pay, allowances, etc.—
   Handbooks, manuals, etc.   I. Title.
   UC74.B84   1996
   331.2'81355'00973—dc20   96-33296
                                                                CIP

CONTENTS

INTRODUCTION

Military Money Guide is about dollars and sense: The dollars that the Pentagon pays for specific purposes and the sensible understanding of how each program works.

It has been written for people who are learning about military programs—new servicemembers, spouses, and other family members. For that reason, jargon is held to a minimum, and subjects are arranged in a commonsense way, as opposed to a by-the-*military*-book system.

That's not to say that veterans have nothing to learn. The military system for paying the troops is littered with informational nuggets that many folks spend a career gathering. *Military Money Guide* offers that detailed, professional information in one place.

The author's thanks go to the real experts in military pay and benefits. They've been helpful in supplying information and patient in the face of efforts to put the regulations into simple English. Any errors are the author's.

Anyone about to make major financial decisions should always make sure he or she has the latest information. Military pay is in constant flux; the regulations for benefits are subject to never-ending tinkering by Congress, the Pentagon, and the services. *Military Money Guide* will provide an overview of programs. Only a face-to-face talk with a military pay expert will provide all the up-to-date details of the programs affecting your finances.

It's important to remember that the patchwork of programs making up the military pay system was created to solve specific problems and rectify inequities that have arisen over the years.

The pay system is there to help military people. And *Military Money Guide* is a tool to ensure that you're taking advantage of everything that's coming to you.

PART ONE

PAY FUNDAMENTALS

ONE

BASIC PAY

In This Chapter:
- *Eligibility*
- *Rates*
- *Pay Raises*

- *Reserves*
- *Special Circumstances*

Basic Pay is the financial foundation upon which every military paycheck is built. Allowances, bonuses, and financial incentives come and go, but active-duty people can count on Basic Pay to show up in their paychecks.

For a military pay program, there's something quite extraordinary about Basic Pay. It's simple. With a few exceptions, if you're on active duty, you draw Basic Pay. When you leave active duty, it stops. Other rules governing Basic Pay are uncommonly straightforward.

ELIGIBILITY

Basic Pay is paid to everyone on active duty in the U.S. military. Reservists also receive Basic Pay when they're officially on active-duty status. Eligibility is unaffected by leave and hospitalization.

Only when an absence from duty involves some sort of misconduct does a servicemember's eligibility for Basic Pay come into question. Ineligible for Basic Pay are people:

• Absent without leave.

• Jailed by sentence of a civilian court.

• Unfit for duty because of alcohol or drug abuse.

Commanders have some latitude in permitting formerly AWOL troops to receive Basic Pay for the period of their absence. Commanders can also take away Basic Pay from people jailed by civilian law authorities while awaiting trial.

Eligibility for Basic Pay continues when military folks are locked up awaiting a court-martial. Even those convicted by a court-martial remain eligible for Basic Pay unless the sentence specifically calls for "forfeiture of pay."

Reservists may be brought on active duty without Basic Pay. That requires their agreement and is covered in more depth in chapter 11, "Reserve Pays."

RATES

The amounts of Basic Pay that active-duty people receive are determined by two factors—the number of years in uniform, plus a person's rank. During 1996, monthly rates for Basic Pay ranged from $809.10 for a recruit to $9,016.80 for a four-star general or admiral.

The amount of Basic Pay isn't decreased when people receive from the military any additional allowance, incentive pay, or bonus, nor is it affected by outside income.

Basic Pay is fully taxable. And it's subject to the legal

process called garnishment, in which a court orders the military to divert money directly from a paycheck to pay someone else, such as a business partner or an ex-spouse.

On the official military pay chart, the years of service are commonly called *fogeys*. With a few specific exceptions, they come every two years—falling on even-numbered years—and end after 26 years.

Two exceptions to the two-year fogey rule are found on the pay chart. First, new recruits, E-1s, have a sort of mini fogey after four months. In 1996, for example, an E-1's Basic Pay rose a hefty 8 percent—from $809.10 monthly to $874.80—after four months in uniform.

The other exception of the two-year fogey rule affects everyone. A fogey after three years' service is the only odd-numbered one on the pay chart.

People who've lost Basic Pay for reasons such as AWOL or court-martial convictions won't have that lost time counted for determining their years of service for pay purposes.

Also for counting years of service, people who come on active duty after serving in the reserves will have that reserve time treated as if it had been active-duty time. The rank used for Basic Pay is the servicemember's official grade. Some services permit people selected for promotion to wear their new, higher rank before the official promotion date. Those frocked ranks don't count for pay purposes.

In 1790, Congress passed a bill authorizing different pay levels for "troops," privates, officers, NCOs, quartermasters, adjutants, and musicians.

Officers in the three lowest commissioned ranks who spent more than four years as warrant officers or enlisted personnel before accepting their commissions have their own Basic Pay categories, commonly displayed as O-1E, O-2E, and O-3E. Once they're promoted to O-4, however, they're treated like everyone else.

PAY RAISES

There are three ways a military member can receive additional Basic Pay:

- By a congressionally approved change in the pay chart.
- By reaching a fogey (discussed in "Rates" above).
- By being promoted.

Whatever the reason, servicemembers don't have to take any action to get extra money.

Pay raises always begin on a specific date. If that date falls within the middle of a month, you're not entitled to the new, higher Basic Pay rate for the entire month, just for the number of days in the month after that date.

If you're entitled to a pay raise for more than one reason—for example, your promotion takes place on the same day you reach a fogey and that happens to be the same day Congress made the pay chart changes—then you get extra money for each of those three reasons.

Let's look a little closer at some of the fine print detailing the rules for the three ways of getting an increase in Basic Pay.

Pay Chart: When most military folks talk about getting a pay raise, they think about the extra money that comes when Congress revises the pay chart for Basic Pay.

Those increases are made by a specified percentage, which applies to all ranks and to all year-of-service fogeys. That same percentage is commonly used to increase the Basic Allowance for Quarters (BAQ) and Basic Allowance for Subsistence (BAS), but Congress can authorize increases of a different percentage.

All E-1s get the same pay after four months in uniform. The same goes for E-2s.

Revisions to the pay chart usually come once a year, and they usually take effect on October 1, which is the start of the federal government's fiscal year.

These are the usual rules, but Congress can rewrite the rules. It can decide not to increase Basic Pay in a year (which happened in 1983 and 1986), or to give more than one pay increase in one year (1972), or to make the increase begin on a date other than October 1.

Years-of-Service (Fogey) Hikes: Typically every two years, military members receive a years-of-service, or fogey, pay raise. That happens when their time in uniform reaches one of the milestones that's recorded along the top of each Basic Pay pay chart.

The timing of these increases is personal. They come when an individual servicemember accumulates the necessary number of years in uniform. Except for those with bad time from AWOL, court-martial conviction, and other causes, a fogey increase will come at the anniversary date of the start of your military career.

The official pay chart has an important word that's omitted from many commercially printed charts. That's the word *over*. The four-year fogey, for example, actually affects folks with *over* four years of military service.

If you joined the military on June 10, 1995, you won't be eligible for your four-year fogey increase until June 11, 1999. In this example, the next pay check will have 10 days' worth of Basic Pay calculated at the rate for people with more than three years' service, and 20 days of Basic Pay computed at the over-four rate.

The size of these years-of-service increases vary, both as a percentage increase in pay and in absolute dollars. In fact, not all ranks get a years-of-service pay raise at each fogey. The pay chart, like much of the military's personnel policy, was designed to nudge folks up the career ladder by not rewarding those who don't advance themselves professionally.

Promotion: The military pay chart has been constructed so that people following normal career progression will get more Basic Pay with each promotion.

Basic Pay at the new, higher rate takes effect on the official date of one's promotion. If your promotion comes on the 11th of the month, you'll get a paycheck reflecting 10 days of pay at the older, lower rank and 20 days at the new rank.

Unofficial promotions—such as being allowed to wear the insignia of a new rank for which you've been approved, although the official promotion date hasn't arrived yet—don't qualify as promotions for pay purposes.

Of course, not everyone follows the normal career progression. Enlisted members can become officers, and despite the higher rank, they may end up qualifying for less Basic Pay.

In those situations, a provision in the regulations called "saved pay" is triggered. It permits enlisted members who become officers to continue getting paid the Basic Pay of their old enlisted rank, if the enlisted rank has more Basic Pay.

Folks affected by saved pay continue to be eligible for the increases they would have gotten if they'd stayed in their enlisted rank. They can switch to the officer rate for Basic Pay whenever they wish, but they cannot receive housing allowances at the officer rate while being paid enlisted Basic Pay under saved pay. They get the housing allowance appropriate for that enlisted rank.

RESERVES

Members of the reserves and National Guard receive Basic Pay when they are officially on:

- Extended active duty.
- Annual training duty.

- Active-duty training.
- Active-duty for training.
- Full-time training duty.
- Temporary active duty.

These kinds of service typically last less than 30 days. Eligible reservists receive Basic Pay only for the number of days they were officially on active duty. Their Basic Pay is calculated to provide one-thirtieth of the monthly Basic Pay rate for each day.

Reservists and National Guardsmen are also entitled to Basic Pay while traveling to the places they serve on active duty. Within the 48 contiguous states, they will usually receive an extra day's Basic Pay at the beginning of that active-duty stint and another day's Basic Pay as they're returning home at the end.

Those two extra days' Basic Pay go to reserve component members traveling to an active-duty station by air. When driving, they must travel at least 525 miles between home and assignment to be credited with more than one day for Basic Pay purposes.

Several categories of service, common to members of the reserve components, expressly *don't* allow anyone to receive Basic Pay. They include:

- Inactive duty for training.
- Active duty without pay.

Sometimes, reserve component members will serve in uniform for periods that are, legally, a mixture of active-duty time and drill time. When that happens, military folks cannot receive Drill Pay on the same day as Basic Pay.

Another tricky spot in the pay regulations for reservists involves retirees recalled to active duty. They cannot draw both Basic Pay and retired pay. But the rules give them some latitude. They can keep whichever pay—Basic Pay or retired pay—is the larger.

For retirees on active duty, accepting Basic Pay doesn't take away any retiree rights, and keeping retired pay doesn't affect any other active-duty benefits, such as eligibility for the Basic Allowance for Quarters.

SPECIAL CIRCUMSTANCES

A variety of factors affects the Basic Pay of military members. Here are some of some of the most commonly encountered ones.

> **P**roblems getting ashore don't justify postdischarge basic pay increase for sailors and Marines.

At Sea after Discharge: It's not always possible for sailors and Marines to get off ships before their enlistments expire. If they're stuck afloat after their formal discharge dates, they continue to get paid everything that made up their paychecks before the arrival of their discharge dates.

If the ship is operating in foreign waters and if the sailor or Marine is kept aboard because the commanding officer formally certifies that their "service is essential to the public interest," then they get a break. They're entitled to receive a 25 percent increase in their Basic Pay.

Demotion: For demoted enlisted folks, the new, lower Basic Pay takes effect on the day shown on the demotion orders.

Most demoted officers are discharged. The only ones retained had erroneous promotions based on administrative errors. They can keep the extra Basic Pay up to what the regulations call "the date of discovery."

Posthumous Promotion: Usually, posthumous promotions don't affect Basic Pay. The exception involves people who were prisoners of war, missing in action or officially in missing status at the time of death.

Retroactive Promotion: Sometimes, the promotion dates of officers are moved back solely for the purpose of giving an officer more (or less) seniority over officers of the same rank.

These retroactive promotions are used to calculate an officer's time in grade when it comes to promotion, but the retroactive date has no effect upon pay.

TWO

BASIC ALLOWANCE
FOR QUARTERS

In This Chapter:
- *Eligibility*
- *Overview on Rates*
- *Tax Status*
- *With-Dependents Rate*
- *Without-Dependents Rate*
- *The Partial Rate*

- *BAQ and On-Base Housing*
- *Dual-Service Couples*
- *BAQ and Reservists*
- *Special Circumstances*

Everyone on active duty is entitled to government housing. The housing must be free, appropriate for the person's rank, and large enough for the family.

The Basic Allowance for Quarters (BAQ) is the major financial supplement going to military members when active-duty people end up paying for their own housing.

Many BAQ recipients also qualify for other housing-related bonuses. Stateside, a majority receive the Variable Housing

Allowance (VHA). Residents of civilian communities overseas commonly receive an addition to BAQ that's called the Overseas Housing Allowance (OHA).

ELIGIBILITY

BAQ can be paid to everyone on active duty, officers and enlisted, single people and those with families, plus reservists on extended active duty.

Usually, BAQ is the *flip-side* of government housing. If you don't have government housing, you should get BAQ. Conversely, if you get government housing, you usually don't get BAQ.

BAQ Summary:	
Purpose:	To pay for off-base housing
Amounts:	$193.50 to $970.50 monthly (1996)
Formula:	By rank, dependents
Taxable:	No
Loopholes:	Some on-base residents get BAQ
Problem Areas:	Divorced or separated with children; lengthy duty in another location; arrest; dual-service couples.

Usually, single people—or, more technically, those without dependents—who are officers, warrant officers, or enlisted people in the rank of E-6 or in a higher enlisted rank can choose whether to live off base and draw BAQ, unless specifically ordered into on-base quarters. This is a rule, not an absolute right.

A variety of other factors—from illnesses and AWOL to duty aboard ship or in the field—can affect BAQ eligibility. These factors are discussed below in the section, entitled "Special Circumstances."

OVERVIEW ON RATES

Each military rank has four different BAQ rates.

- One for people with family members who officially qualify as dependents.
- A second for military folks without dependents.
- A third for service members living in barracks, aboard ship or during field exercises, called the partial rate.
- A fourth, called BAQ-Diff, for divorced military members whose only dependent is a child living with an ex-spouse.

The first three BAQ rates are part of the regular military pay chart. The fourth, BAQ-Diff, is calculated by a simple formula: Subtract a servicemember's BAQ at the without-dependents rate from that same person's BAQ at the with-dependents rate.

During 1996, BAQ at the with-dependents level ranged from $345.60 monthly for a new recruit to $970.50 for a four-star general or admiral. The without-dependents rate started at $193.50 monthly for the E-1 and topped out at $788.40 for O-10s.

The partial rate usually received by people in barracks or aboard ship started in 1996 at $6.90 monthly for a recruit and ranged to $50.70 for a four-star officer.

The actual cost of off-base housing doesn't affect BAQ payments. Everyone receiving BAQ receives the maximum rate given the rules affecting their dependents.

BAQ rates are usually paid a month at a time, but sometimes payments shrink to a daily rate, which is one-thirtieth the monthly rate.

Causing a shift to a daily rate could be gaining your first official dependent by marriage or birth; losing your last official dependent by divorce, death, or a child's 21st birthday; or moving into government quarters or moving out of them.

TAX STATUS

BAQ is tax-free. That applies to state and federal income taxes, as well as taxes for Social Security and Medicare.

This tax protection applies equally to the four different BAQ rates—the with-dependents rate, the without-dependents rate, the partial rate, and BAQ-Diff.

The tax-free nature of BAQ is unaffected by its use. For example, interest paid on mortgages to buy homes is tax deductible. Using tax-free BAQ money to pay for a tax-deductible mortgage seems like more of a break than the IRS can tolerate, but it's perfectly legal.

THE WITH-DEPENDENTS RATE

If a family member is living with you off base—or living elsewhere, but with you supporting him or her financially—then you probably qualify for BAQ at the larger, with-dependents rate.

Having just one other person in the household triggers eligibility for with-dependents BAQ. But it can't be just anyone. That other person must meet the military's official definition of dependent, which includes the following people:

Spouses: The spouse doesn't have to live with the servicemember, but the spouse must be legally recognized and the military member must financially support the spouse. For more on troubled marriages, see "Special Circumstances" below.

Parents: Military members with no other dependents can qualify for BAQ at the with-dependents rate if they provide at least half of their parents' income. This includes stepparents, but not in-laws.

Children: There's no question about the children of servicemembers qualifying as dependents if they meet all of the following conditions in one of the following categories:

• They're legitimate, 20 years of age or younger, and living with the military member.

• They're legitimate, 22 years of age or younger, and enrolled in a full-time course of education.

• Regardless of age, they're incapable of supporting themselves because of a physical or mental disability that began when they were a dependent, and they receive at least half of their financial support from the servicemember.

• They're legally adopted children, stepchildren living with the military member who receive at least half their financial support from that active-duty person, or illegitimate children when the military person has admitted being the parent or a court has formally decreed that the uniformed person is the parent.

A special case involves the child of a divorced servicemember who lives with the civilian parent and who receives child-support payments from the military parent. If that child is the only dependent of the military person, the BAQ-Diff rate applies.

Military folks entitled to BAQ-Diff can receive the extra money when they live on base in government quarters. But in those cases, the child-support payment must be at least as large as the BAQ-Diff rate. Military folks in that category living off base receive BAQ at the without-dependents rate, plus the BAQ-Diff rate.

THE PARTIAL RATE

Many military people without dependents are eligible for a small BAQ payment when they live in quarters provided by the government. These BAQ payments are made at the "partial rate."

Recipients include servicemembers without dependents who live in barracks, dormitories, aboard ship, or in the field.

Sometimes, people with dependents find themselves living

in those facilities. They don't get partial-rate BAQ. Instead, they continue receiving BAQ at the with-dependents rate.

Often, lower-ranking enlisted personnel without dependents choose to live off base, and their commanders don't order them to move into government quarters. Instead, they'll be carried on the books as being assigned to government quarters but not occupying government quarters.

In this case, because they're officially assigned to (unoccupied) government quarters, they're eligible for partial BAQ and ineligible for BAQ at the without-dependents rate.

BAQ AND ON-BASE HOUSING

When on-base quarters are officially designated as "inadequate," military families can still move in—and the active-duty person can receive at least 25 percent of the usual monthly BAQ at the with-dependents rate.

Also receiving BAQ—momentarily—are people who live on base at installations with housing constructed under a number of post-World War II construction programs.

Residents of those homes receive BAQ from the military, which they pay to their civilian landlords for rent. (The original contracts for those housing developments stipulate that the rent shouldn't exceed BAQ.)

DUAL-SERVICE COUPLES

When husband and wife are both on active duty, special care (and extra confusion) are involved in sorting out the status of their BAQ. Some inconsistencies lurk in the rule book.

The pay regulations discuss more than two dozen different kinds of circumstances affecting BAQ rates

Dual-service couples should proceed with caution when trying to claim each other as a dependent.

for dual-service couples. Here are the rules for the more common situations:

• *No other dependents, living in a civilian community, neither spouse officially assigned to single, on-base housing:* Both spouses would receive BAQ at the without-dependents rate.

• *At least one child or another dependent, living in civilian community, neither spouse assigned to single, on-base housing:* One spouse would receive BAQ at the with-dependents rate, the other at the without-dependents rate.

• *No other dependents, both spouses officially assigned to single, on-base housing:* Both spouses would receive partial BAQ.

• *No other dependent, one spouse assigned to single, on-base housing but living off base:* On-base spouse would receive partial BAQ; the off-base spouse would be paid without-dependents BAQ.

• *At least one child or another official dependent, living in civilian community but with one spouse assigned to single, on-base housing:* One spouse would be paid BAQ at the with-dependents rate; the other would receive partial BAQ.

BAQ AND RESERVISTS
Members of the reserves and National Guard can qualify for BAQ payments when they are on active duty. Whether they're paid at the with-dependents rate or the without-dependents rate relies upon having family members who meet the official definition of dependents.

Here are some special situations affecting reservists and their eligibility for BAQ:

• When on regular once-a-month "drill status," they're not entitled to any BAQ money.

• When on active duty—whether for several years or an annual 14-day training period—they're treated like any other

BAQ recipient. (A 14-day stretch on active duty during the summer will result in fourteen-thirtieths of the monthly BAQ rate.)

• National Guardsmen who have been called up by their states for disaster relief or some other emergencies don't receive BAQ. That may change if the federal government takes over operations.

Reservists and National Guardsmen without dependents who are called to duty for "a contingency operation"—which can include temporary wartime service, disaster relief, or law enforcement—can receive BAQ at the without-dependents rate, even though the government is providing a bed and a roof overhead.

These reservists must be able to prove they have a financial responsibility to maintain their original homes. In most cases, a rental contract or a mortgage agreement proves that responsibility.

SPECIAL CIRCUMSTANCES

Here's how the regulations treat military folks in several other special circumstances:

Afield/Afloat: Military people with dependents keep their BAQ at the with-dependents level when assigned to field duty or sea duty.

If you meet all three of the following conditions—on sea duty, E-5 or lower rank, and don't have official dependents—then you can lose BAQ during sea duty.

If assigned to field duty, in most cases, you'd keep your BAQ at the without-dependents rate.

AWOL: When E-1s, E-2s, E-3s, and E-4s with less than four years' service are absent without leave, their spouses can request a direct payment of two months' BAQ.

Spouses cannot apply until the active-duty person has been

absent for at least 29 days; they also cannot apply after the military member has been officially absent for more than three months. For servicemembers whose only dependent is an under-aged child, applications can be made on the child's behalf by a guardian.

Ineligible for these direct payments are spouses who are living in government quarters. The dependents of higher-ranking enlisted members and officers cannot claim direct payment of BAQ if their servicemembers are absent without leave.

Boyfriends/Girlfriends: To qualify for BAQ at the with-dependents rate, military folks must have at least one other person in the household who officially qualifies as a dependent. Live-in boyfriends and girlfriends, even when totally dependent financially upon the military member, aren't dependents.

Divorce and Separation: A spouse from whom a military member is legally or even informally separated can still be a dependent, so long as he or she is still financially supported by the military member. How much support is enough? Usually, the spouse must receive at least as much money as the member's BAQ payment.

As a rock-bottom minimum, the spouse must receive at least the BAQ-Diff amount.

Once a divorce is official, then the spouse is no longer an official military dependent. Paying alimony to an ex-spouse won't enable anyone to get BAQ at the with-dependents rate, nor will the payment of money for a community property settlement.

Divorce and Children: Military members need only one official dependent to qualify for BAQ at the with-dependents rate. Sometimes, the only way they can qualify is by having at least one child who lives with an ex-spouse.

As with spouses during separations, the servicemember must financially support the child. That support, at a minimum, must equal the amount of money left after subtracting someone's BAQ at the without-dependents rate from that same person's BAQ at the with-dependents rate.

Servicemembers receiving BAQ whose only dependent is a child receiving child support receive BAQ-Diff, not BAQ at the with-dependents rate.

When the child stays with the military parent, the child must stay for a continuous period of more than 90 days in order for the servicemember to receive BAQ at the with-dependents rate.

Garnishment: BAQ is protected from collection by people to whom military folks owe money—specifically, any debts to businesses or for child support and alimony.

Hospitalization: Servicemembers drawing BAQ at the with-dependents rate continue to receive it when hospitalized.

Active-duty folks without dependents can lose their BAQ if they're formally assigned to the hospital for treatment.

Jail: Servicemembers receiving partial-rate BAQ generally will continue to receive it when they are confined to a guardhouse, brig, correctional barracks, rehabilitation facility, or their own quarters. That's the general rule. But they can lose partial-rate BAQ if that's specifically ordered by the proper military authority.

Nonsupport of Family: BAQ has a with-dependents rate so military people can provide housing for their families. If servicemembers don't support their families, the military will order them to repay their BAQ.

Commanders can insist upon proof of support before they authorize BAQ to resume.

POWs and MIAs: Servicemembers who become prisoners of war, who are listed as missing in action, or who are imprisoned in a foreign country continue being credited with BAQ at the with-dependents or without-dependents rate throughout their captivity.

If they were receiving partial BAQ when captured, their BAQ is automatically switched to the without-dependents rate. POWs, MIAs, and prisoners get the advantage of increases in BAQ rates. They're also eligible for promotions, which lead to more BAQ.

Reassignments: Military members with PCS orders can occupy temporary government quarters for less than 30 days without losing their BAQ payments. Commanders can authorize periods longer than 30 days, with full BAQ.

Temporary Duty: Servicemembers drawing BAQ at the with-dependents rate continue to receive it during stints of temporary duty (TDY) and temporary additional duty (TAD).

People without dependents who are E-6s and lower rank lose BAQ during TDY and TAD periods if assigned to government quarters at their permanent duty station. The key word is *assigned*. Some folks are technically assigned to government quarters, but they live off base.

E-7s, E-8s, E-9s, and all officers keep their BAQ at the without-dependents rate during TDY and TAD periods, even if they occupy government quarters during those periods.

THREE

BASIC ALLOWANCE FOR SUBSISTENCE

In This Chapter:
- *Eligibility*
- *Overview on Rates*
- *Rules*
- *Supplemental Subsistence Allowance*
- *Prorated Subsistence Allowance*
- *Tax Status*
- *Special Circumstances*

If the military isn't providing meals directly to a member of the armed forces, the military usually provides the Basic Allowance for Subsistence (BAS), a financial payment that enables active-duty people to purchase their own food.

It's always prudent to make sure you have current information about rates and rules for any major element of a military paycheck before making financial decisions. BAS is an area especially worthy of caution.

ELIGIBILITY

BAS can be paid to everyone on active duty, officer and enlisted, single people and those with families, plus reservists and National Guardsmen on extended active duty. Except in rare circumstances, officers always receive it. In the enlisted ranks, married folks and single people in the ranks of E-7, E-8, and E-9 can usually count on having BAS payments in their paychecks.

For enlisted personnel, a factor in determining BAS eligibility is the availability of a government dining facility. If the government can feed them, then the government usually won't pay them.

Still, both things can happen at the same time. More about this is included in the section entitled "Special Cases," below.

OVERVIEW ON RATES

BAS rates fall into two major categories—one for officers, the other for enlisted. Officers have only one rate. Enlisted BAS falls into three major categories, plus two additional categories that are less common.

For all commissioned officers and warrant officers, BAS is $149.67 monthly (1996).

When an officer is fed by the government—in unit "messes," MREs, aboard ship, or in a hospital—the officer has to pay for the meal. The amount of that payment is set by each service.

Officers in the field can receive, in addition to BAS, a payment called per diem that offsets some costs for food.

Enlisted rates are normally expressed as a daily amount. All the enlisted rates—and many of the enlisted rules—come in two sizes, one for folks with less than four months in uniform and a second one for everyone else.

Keeping this dividing line in mind, there are three basic

BAS Summary:	
Purpose:	Pay for food away from government facilities
Amounts:	For officers, $149.67 monthly (1996) For enlisted, from $6.59 to $10.67 daily (1996)
Formula:	None for officers, complicated system for enlisteds
Taxable:	No
Loopholes:	Can draw BAS and per diem
Problem Areas:	On leave, drawing per diem

kinds of BAS, plus two other kinds that are essentially add-ons. They have cumbersome titles:

• "Rations in kind not available."

• "On leave or granted permission to mess separately" (known informally as "sep-rats").

• "Emergency conditions where no government messing is available."

The two add-on categories involve situations in which enlisted people eat some meals in a government dining facility and some in homes, restaurants, or fast-food stores:

• "Prorated Subsistence Allowance."

• "Supplemental Subsistence Allowance."

Each service has its own rules for determining what category of BAS applies in which kinds of cases. Installation commanders and theater commanders with more than one service under their command can impose uniform BAS rules for their bases.

BAS rates are set by Congress. Usually, rates increase every year at the same time as the military pay raise and by the same amount. Congress can vote for BAS to increase by amounts greater or smaller than the Basic Pay hike.

RULES

"On Leave or Granted Permission to Mess Separately":
This is the category of BAS that enlisted people receive most often, the one when they're married, or living off base or living on base with enough rank that they don't have to eat in military dining halls.

People in all these situations have, as the name of the BAS category states, "permission to mess separately" by their commander or by the regulations of their service. This kind of BAS has the nickname of "separate rations," and the nickname has the nickname of "sep-rats".

In 1996, enlisted folks receiving BAS under this provision got $6.59 daily if they had less than four months in the military, and $7.15 daily if they had more time.

Separate-rations BAS also goes to enlisted people who are on leave, pass, or liberty, are hospitalized or are on certain kinds of official "travel status." The travel status rules affect people on official travel, temporary duty, or traveling to a new permanent assignment—all of whom draw "per diem" while retaining BAS.

BAS at the separate-rations rate doesn't go to anyone under military legal action, even if acquitted.

Since 1994, recipients of separate-rations BAS kept the money if they met both of the following rules:

• They were being fed in a government mess or on field rations.

• They were serving with troops on maneuvers, war games, field exercises, or similar operations.

Note that this definition doesn't include actual combat operations or sea duty. As this book went to press, enlisted personnel lost their separate-rations BAS when they went into a combat zone or embarked for sea duty.

"Rations in Kind Not Available": When there's simply no government dining facility where enlisted folks can be fed, this is the category of BAS they receive.

In 1996, it amounted to $7.43 daily for people with less than four months on active duty, and $8.06 daily for those with more time in service.

> One of the first laws on military pay in 1790 set the pattern that money for "rations" wasn't included in "pay."

This category of BAS mainly goes to enlisted people who work off base. If a government dining hall is available for some meals, then BAS under this category will be reduced to take into consideration the meals that the military provides.

BAS under this category doesn't go to servicemembers who are traveling to a new duty assignment, even though they might not be able to eat in a government dining hall. Those cases are covered above in "On Leave or When Granted Permission to Mess Separately."

Often, a government dining facility is officially "unavailable" if it's more than 30 minutes away from the place a military person works. That's a rough guideline. Installation commanders and unit commanders have considerable discretion in making decisions affecting eligibility for this kind of enlisted BAS.

"Emergency Conditions Where No Government Messing Is Available": Sometimes enlisted people find themselves in places where government-provided food isn't available and the usual BAS rate doesn't come close to paying for food.

For situations like this, the government has established a special category of enlisted BAS. It's also known as the Emergency Ration Rate, or ERR.

B AS was designed to pay for food for the servicemember, not for the servicemember's family.

For 1996, the rates allowed $9.86 daily for an enlisted person with less than four months' service, and $10.67 daily for everyone else. Only a narrow set of circumstances justifies this benefit:

• The enlisted member has a temporary assignment expected to last less than 180 days.

• The assignment is within one of the 48 contiguous states.

• Government dining facilities are unavailable.

• The service member's room doesn't have cooking facilities.

• Payment has been approved in advance by the service.

SUPPLEMENTAL SUBSISTENCE ALLOWANCE

Sometimes, enlisted members are consistently unable to use a government dining facility because there's none near their place of duty. Enlisted members given separate-rations BAS can sometimes qualify for an additional payment for each meal that they must pay for out of their own pocket.

Called the Supplemental Subsistence Allowance, it has different rates for breakfast, lunch, and dinner. The rates are small, amounting in 1995 to less than 50 cents per meal.

PRORATED SUBSISTENCE ALLOWANCE

When an enlisted member with BAS eats in a government dining hall, that person cannot collect BAS for that meal. The prorated subsistence allowance is the amount of BAS that a servicemember gets after having the cost of that meal deducted from the daily BAS rate.

The amount of that loss depends upon the meal and the kind of BAS being drawn. Someone with separate-rations BAS won't lose the same amount of money for eating breakfast in the mess hall as a person drawing emergency-rations BAS who has the same meal in the same place.

The per-meal rates are calculated in such as way that people eating three meals a day in a government mess hall for a month will pay 100 percent of their BAS, regardless of the kind of BAS they've been receiving.

TAX STATUS

BAS is tax-free. That applies to state and federal income taxes, as well as taxes for Social Security and Medicare. This tax protection applies equally to the different BAS rates.

The tax-free nature of BAS is unaffected by any use you might put it to. It's supposed to be for food. But if you use it to pay for clothes, a car, or beer, that's your decision.

SPECIAL CIRCUMSTANCES

BAS has more subtleties in its rules than many types of military pay that involve more money. Here's how the rules apply in various circumstances:

Advance Payments: BAS payments may be made in advance. The maximum is three months' BAS. Repayment is made by losing all BAS in later months until the advance has been paid back. Advance payments require a commander's approval.

Afloat: Officers keep their BAS during sea duty, although they must pay for their shipboard meals.

Enlisted members lose BAS during sea duty because the government is feeding them. As this book went to press, the sea-going services were under pressure to let enlisted folks on sea duty keep their BAS.

Rules for BAS afloat are under pressure by lawmakers. Make sure you have the latest details.

AWOL: All servicemembers—officers and enlisted—who have unauthorized absences lose BAS.

Excess Leave: When military folks have used all of their annual vacation but they've received permission to be away from their duties, they're said to be on "excess leave." Both officers and enlisted members lose BAS while they're on excess leave.

Garnishment: BAS is protected from collection by people to whom military folks owe money—specifically, any debts to businesses or for child support and alimony.

Hospitalization: Officers who are hospitalized in a government facility continue to receive their regular BAS, although they may be charged for their food.

All enlisted members receive BAS at the separate-rations rate while hospitalized. Like officers, they may be charged for each meal.

Jail: Officers who are confined continue to receive their BAS, although they may have to pay the government for the meals they are served. They can continue to receive BAS after being convicted by a court-martial unless the sentence of the court specifically requires them to forfeit "allowances."

Enlisted people lose their BAS as soon as they come into official custody.

Leave: Officers continue to receive their monthly BAS payments while on leave.

Enlisted members receive BAS at the separate-rations rate while on leave. BAS for leave time ends, officially, at midnight after the last day on leave.

Overseas COLA: Overseas Cost-of-Living Allowances (COLAs) have no effect on BAS. You won't lose anything from your BAS because you collect an Overseas COLA. Nor will your BAS rate affect the amount of the COLA. (For more information, see chapter 9, "Overseas Pays.")

Per Diem: Military personnel can receive both BAS and Per Diem. Generally, enlisted people drawing per diem receive BAS at the separate-rations rate.

POWs and MIAs: Servicemembers listed as prisoners of war or missing in action are credited with BAS payments. Enlisted members will be credited with BAS at the separate-rations rate.

Reserves: Reservists and National Guardsmen who are officially "ordered to active duty *without* pay" can receive BAS at the regular rates at their permanent duty stations. Rates drop to a token payment—$1.50 per meal in 1995—for meals consumed away from the permanent duty station.

Reservists and National Guardsmen on active duty "without pay *and allowances*" are ineligible for BAS.

Reservists and guardsmen are ineligible for BAS during inactive-duty training, as the monthly drill periods are called.

FOUR

TAXES

Members of the U.S. military are also members of U.S. society. With citizenship comes certain responsibility. Or, to put it more bluntly, if you wear a uniform, you still pay the tax man.

Some kinds of military pay—generally, those officially called "allowances"—are free from federal and state income taxes. A very specific kind of combat-related service will protect some income from taxes.

What follows is a summary, not a compilation, of everything

you may need to know. Keep in mind that tax law, especially state-tax law, is always changing. Make sure you're basing your financial future on the latest version of all the facts.

THREE RULES ON TAXABILITY

First, military pay is generally taxable. That applies to federal income taxes, state income taxes, Social Security taxes, and Medicare taxes. That's true for active-duty pay, reserve pay, and retired pay. But like many rules, it has exceptions:

- Taxes are never paid on some parts of the military paycheck.
- In certain combat zones, military folks get some tax relief.

Second, if the federal government *doesn't* tax a particular type of military pay, neither will the states.

Third, you don't need a financial planner to take advantage of the nontaxable kinds of military pay. The military makes it very easy.

If you've been receiving a nontaxable kind of military pay, that money is simply not included by the government on your W-2 Form, "Wage and Tax Statement," the annual summary of your wages that you get to fill out your income tax forms.

TAXABLE AND NONTAXABLE INCOME

In peacetime, certain elements of a military paycheck are always taxable and others are always nontaxable. Here are the kinds of military pay that are always taxable:

- Aviation Career Incentive Pay.
- Aviator Retention Bonus.
- Basic Pay.
- Career Sea Pay.
- Chemical Munitions Pay.
- Continuation Pay for Aviation Officers.
- Dangerous Organisms Lab Duty Pay.
- Diving Pay.

- Demolition Duty Pay.
- Enlistment Bonuses.
- Experimental Stress Duty Pay.
- Flight Deck Duty Pay.
- Foreign Duty Pay.
- Foreign Language Proficiency Pay.
- Hazardous Duty Pays.
- Hostile Fire Pay.
- Imminent Danger Pay.
- Inactive-duty Pay (or Drill Pay).
- Leave Pay.
- Leave time (cashed in).
- Parachute Pay.
- Reenlistment bonuses.
- Retired Pay (nondisability).
- Sea Duty Pay.
- Separation Pay.
- Special Duty Assignment Pay.
- Special pay for Nurse Corps officers.
- Special Separation Benefit.
- Submarine Pay.
- Toxic Fuels Pay.
- Toxic Pesticides Pay.
- Voluntary Separation Incentive.

On the other side of the coin, the following kinds of military pay are always nontaxable:

- Basic Allowance for Quarters.
- Basic Allowance for Subsistence.
- Clothing Allowance.
- Family Separation Allowance.
- Move-In Housing Allowance.
- Per Diem.
- Overseas Cost-of-Living Allowance.

- Overseas Housing Allowance.
- Travel Allowance.
- Travel reimbursements.
- Uniform Allowance.
- Variable Housing Allowance.

Also in the nontaxable category are some important benefits that have a cash value. Military medicine, meals in a military dining facility, commissaries, exchanges, government housing, and other on-base services—these are the kinds of job-related "freebies" that civilians can pay taxes on.

There are also payments *from* military folks that have tax consequences. These payments are subtracted from paychecks before the finance center figures taxes. In this group are payments for the following:

- Dependent Dental Plan.
- Montgomery GI Bill.
- Servicemen's Group Life Insurance.
- Survivor Benefit Plan.

The tax status of at least two kinds of military pay may or may not be taxable, depending upon a variety of factors. These include:

- Disability retired pay.
- Disability severance pay.

COMBAT ZONE EXCLUSION

With the stroke of a pen, the president of the United States has the authority to set some of the pay of military folks beyond the reach of the tax man. This is called the combat zone exclusion.

Federal and state income taxes are eliminated—or limited— by this measure, but Social Security and Medicare taxes continue to be collected.

Almost everyone eligible for the combat zone exclusion receives Hostile Fire Pay or Imminent Danger Pay. But only a small portion of the people receiving Hostile Fire Pay and Imminent Danger Pay are shielded from the IRS.

Since the end of the Vietnam War, only the Persian Gulf War and peacekeeping operations in Bosnia have resulted in creation of a combat zone exclusion for military taxpayers.

Amounts: Commissioned officers have a fixed amount of their monthly military pay shielded from federal and state income tax for each month they're covered by the combat zone exclusion. Until 1995, that protected amount was $500 monthly. Beginning November 21, 1995, the first $4,254.90 of monthly pay for officers is tax-exempt.

For enlisted members and warrant officers, all of their military paychecks are protected from federal and state income taxes for each month they're in the official combat zone.

One day in the designated area triggers a full month's benefit from the combat zone exclusion.

The combat zone exclusion doesn't protect income that's earned by military members from sources *outside* the combat zone, such as investments and dividends.

The Zone: Each executive order or federal law authorizing the combat zone exclusion gives a very precise definition for the geographic area affected. For the Persian Gulf War, the combat zone included the following areas:

• Bahrain, Iraq, Kuwait, Qatar, Oman, Saudi Arabia, and the United Arab Emirates.

• The Persian Gulf, Red Sea, Gulf of Oman, and Gulf of Aden.

• The portion of the Arabian Sea that lies north of 10 degrees north latitude and west of 68 degrees east longitude.

Combat in Panama, Grenada, Somalia, and Haiti didn't qualify for combat zone tax protection.

For troops in the former Yugoslavia, the zone includes Bosnia, Croatia, and Macedonia.

The combat zone includes the airspace above the designated countries and waters adjacent to their shores.

Service in the Zone: Generally, if you're assigned to the combat zone and you're physically present there, then you qualify for the combat zone exclusion.

It doesn't matter whether you're active-duty military or a reservist. Nor is it important whether you arrived on temporary duty or with permanent-change-of-station (PCS) orders.

In fact, some people who aren't physically present in the combat zone qualify for this tax protection. They include people who receive Hostile Fire Pay or Imminent Danger Pay and who also meet one of the following descriptions:

• Servicemembers outside the zone who launch cruise missiles toward targets inside the zone.

• Ground crews who load and maintain aircraft that fly into the combat zone.

• People outside the combat zone who support other members of their unit or installation on combat operations.

Not eligible for combat zone protections are military people assigned outside the zone who travel into it while on leave. Also not eligible are crewmembers and passengers aboard aircraft and naval vessels traveling between two points outside the zone who pass through the region during their trip.

FEDERAL TAXES

Like other taxpayers, military members must ensure that money is withheld from each paycheck to meet their tax obligations. Also like other taxpayers, military people can increase or decrease their amount of that withholding to take into account their personal circumstances. Finance offices have the proper forms to adjust the amount of withholdings.

When military members fail to pay their federal taxes, the Internal Revenue Service can use special administrative procedures that permit collection of delinquent taxes directly from the military finance center.

In extreme cases, the IRS can collect portions of a military paycheck that are normally tax exempt, such as housing allowances or travel reimbursements. They can even collect money the servicemember has designated for other purposes, like payments for life insurance or the Montgomery GI Bill.

WHAT'S YOUR STATE?

Everyone in the military is a legal resident of one of the 50 states, the District of Columbia, the territory of Puerto Rico, another U.S. possession, or a foreign country.

Your tax responsibility is toward the state that's your legal residence. In the military, you can avoid paying the state income taxes in the state where you're stationed if it's not your legal residence.

On the other hand, the state that is your legal residence can collect state income taxes from you, regardless of where the military has sent you.

The term *legal residence* is a specific legal entity. It doesn't have to be the state where you grew up, or where you came on active duty. It doesn't have to be the state where the military has assigned you. It doesn't necessarily have to be anywhere you've actually lived.

How do you establish your legal residence? By filling out a form. You already completed one when you came on active duty. If you want to change it, personnel centers and finance office have the proper paperwork, DD Form 2058, *State of Legal Residence Certificate.*

But be warned. That form won't make you a legal resident of one state if you're acting as if you're a resident of another. Buying a home, registering to vote, or registering a car can establish (or change) your legal residence. So will an off-base, after-duty job.

Changing your legal residence, especially to claim a state that doesn't have state income taxes, can be tricky. Check with a military lawyer in advance.

A further warning involves your spouse and dependents. Your legal residence may be one state and your family may have another. This commonly happens when family members work.

STATE TAXES

If a certain kind of military pay is protected from federal taxes, then it can't be taxed by a state, either. Only one state can tax the military income of each servicemember.

If you pay state income taxes, then you also must make regular withholdings from your military paycheck to pay those taxes. Finance centers have the details about how much pay to withhold for each state.

Check with a lawyer before claiming to be a resident of a state in which you don't live, or never have lived.

The following states don't have a personal income tax:
- Alaska.
- Nevada.
- South Dakota.
- Texas.
- Washington.
- Wyoming.

States that don't tax wages (such as a military paycheck) but do tax such things as capital gains, interest payments, stock dividends, or the value of such property as stocks and bonds are the following:
- Florida.

- New Hampshire.
- Tennessee.

These states don't tax a military paycheck:

- Illinois.
- Michigan.
- Montana.

These states won't tax a military paycheck if you're a legal resident and the military has stationed you outside the state:

- Pennsylvania.
- Vermont.

Keep in mind that we've been talking about state income taxes that are applied against a military paycheck. If you're moonlighting, that income is fully taxable by the state, regardless of legal residence.

SOCIAL SECURITY AND MEDICARE

Military members pay taxes to both Social Security and Medicare, and they're eligible to receive benefits from both systems.

Social Security and Medicare taxes are automatically withheld from each military paycheck, using standard government formulas. Having an after-hours job in the civilian sector, for which Social Security and Medicare taxes are also withheld, doesn't affect the amounts of the taxes withheld by the military.

Reservists and National Guardsmen receiving Drill Pay, technically known as Inactive-Duty Pay, have both taxes automatically withheld from those paychecks.

Military retirees are eligible to receive Social Security and Medicare benefits. Military retired pay is free from Social Security and Medicare taxes.

The combat zone exclu-

> In early 1996, Vietnam still qualified as a combat zone for protection from income tax.

sion doesn't protect military income from Social Security and Medicare taxes.

Military pay earned during periods of illness, hospitalization, and absence from duty for medical reasons is still subject to Social Security and Medicare taxes.

Contributions to the Montgomery GI Bill aren't subject to Social Security or Medicare taxes. Servicemembers who lose their Basic Pay because of a court-martial sentence, an AWOL stint, or confinement in a civilian jail don't have to pay Social Security or Medicare taxes on the military pay they didn't receive.

RESERVISTS

Reservists and National Guardsmen on active duty are covered by the same federal and state tax laws as anyone else on active duty.

Inactive-Duty Pay, more commonly called Drill Pay, is subject to federal taxes. Treatment of Drill Pay by state income tax agencies varies from state to state.

MILITARY RETIREES

Military retired pay is considered taxable income. Except in the case of some disabled military retirees, people collecting military retired pay must pay federal income taxes.

States can tax military retired pay. We'll review later in this section the general rules about state taxation of military retired pay.

Social Security and Medicare taxes aren't collected from any military retired pay. Military retirees can receive Social Security and Medicare benefits without having that affect their retired pay. By the same standard, their military retired pay doesn't affect their right to receive benefits from Social Security and Medicare.

Military retirees who live outside the United States are still subject to federal income tax and are required to have monthly withholdings of their taxes.

There are some narrowly drawn exceptions to the taxability of military retired pay:

• Retirees with disabilities related to injuries or illnesses incurred in combat.

• Retirees entitled to receive military disability retired pay on September 24, 1975, or at an earlier date.

• Retirees who were on active duty or within a reserve component on September 24, 1975, or at an earlier date.

Several specific deductions are made from military retired pay before the finance centers compute a retiree's tax obligations. This has the effect of lowering the amount of income you pay taxes upon. These include the following:

• Contributions to the Survivor Benefit Plan.

• Reductions of retired pay under the Dual Compensation Act, which affects retirees who take second jobs as federal civil servants.

• Contributions to the old Retired Serviceman's Family Protection Plan, an early version of SBP.

• Waivers of retired pay to collect VA disability compensation.

This leaves state income taxes, as they apply to military retirees. These states don't have any personal income tax:

• Alaska.
• Nevada.
• South Dakota.
• Texas.
• Washington.
• Wyoming.

These states don't tax any military retired pay:

• Alabama.

- Florida.
- Hawaii.
- Kansas.
- Kentucky.
- Louisiana.
- Michigan.
- Nevada.
- New York.
- Pennsylvania.
- Tennessee.

These states give a tax break to military retirees:

- Arkansas.
- Colorado.
- Delaware
- District of Columbia.
- Illinois.
- Indiana.
- Maryland.
- Mississippi.
- North Carolina.
- Ohio.
- Oklahoma.
- Oregon.
- South Carolina.

States that aren't included in any of the listings above treat military retired pay the same as any other source of income.

Collection of state income taxes has become a controversial issue in recent years. The code phrase is "source tax." It's easiest to explain by example:

A servicemember with a legal residence in Maine spends a total of 5 years in Nevada during a 20-year military career. When that servicemember retires, Nevada says that a quarter of the person's retired pay is subject to Nevada income taxes because a quarter of the person's military career was spent in Nevada.

So far, military finance centers have refused to honor a request filed by any state for a "source tax."

A final warning: Some retirees have tried to take the "source tax" formula and apply it to the "combat zone exclusion." Their thinking works something like this:

If someone spent 2 years during a 20-year career in a duly designated combat zone, that's 10 percent of a military career. Then, they argue, 10 percent of that person's retired pay should be shielded from all taxes, because it was earned in a combat zone, where military pay is shielded from all taxes.

That argument hasn't been accepted by the courts. Legal experts say it's unlikely to be.

SPECIAL CIRCUMSTANCES

Some situations that military people can find themselves in also have tax consequences. Here are a few special cases:

Deaths: When people die, the survivors administering their estates are responsible for ensuring that income taxes are paid on the money earned during the year of the death.

But for the military, there are three specific instances in which people who die on active duty are exempt from taxes on their last calendar year's income. These tax-exempt groups are:

• Deaths in a combat zone.
• Deaths from terrorism.
• Deaths from "military action overseas."

Hospitalization: The full tax-shielding provisions of the combat zone exclusion apply to hospitalized servicemembers, regardless of the place of hospitalization, if they were hurt in an official combat zone.

Several points are important:

• This applies only to military people hurt in a combat zone established under the combat zone exclusion rules.

• This applies equally to those people wounded in combat, sickened by a virus, or injured by a piece of equipment.

• This applies only to the hospitalized. If you're not living 24 hours a day in a hospital, it doesn't apply to you.

• This provision only applies to military folks. If you're discharged, you lose this tax protection, even if you remain hospitalized from combat-zone injuries.

• Normally, this tax protection ends two years after the formal end of a conflict.

Non-Resident Aliens: Nonresident aliens in the U.S. military are subject to federal income taxes while serving within one of the 50 states or upon U.S. coastal waters. Whether they're subject to state income taxes depends on state law.

For service outside the United States, nonresident aliens aren't subject to federal income tax or any state income tax. This tax protection also includes periods within the United States that last less than 60 days.

POWs and MIAs: The families of military personnel who are classified as prisoners of war or missing in action continue to receive the military member's paycheck, tax free.

The tax exemption is measured in months. It doesn't extend to people who are missing in a combat zone whom the military doesn't classify as either POW or MIA.

Puerto Rico: When serving in the U.S. military, people who are legal residents of Puerto Rico don't pay federal income tax on their military wages. The Puerto Rican government has an income tax of its own, however, and Puerto Ricans in the U.S. military pay it.

COLLECTION

The government can order military finance centers to send portions of a delinquent tax payer's military paycheck straight to an IRS office.

It all begins if a military member receives a formal IRS

notice to pay overdue federal taxes. If the military person hasn't satisfied the tax collector within 30 days, then the government will order the finance center to start collecting the money from a person's military paycheck.

The only way to avoid collection is to be:

> The military is an arm of the government. So are the courts. The military abides by court orders.

• Serving in a combat zone that meets the meaning of the combat zone exclusion.

• Serving immediately outside an official combat zone and drawing Imminent Danger Pay or Hostile Fire Pay.

• Hospitalized because of injuries, illnesses, or wounds incurred in an area meeting the combat zone exclusion definition.

• Listed as missing.

For someone falling into one of these four categories, the collection begins 180 days after the servicemember leaves the combat zone, leaves the hospital, or returns from being missing.

Servicemembers who retire with a debt to the IRS can continue to make regular monthly payments from their retired pay. Others who simply leave the military are liable to see their last paycheck withheld by the government to satisfy the tax collector.

FIVE

CHANGES TO PAY

In This Chapter:
- *Advance Pay*
- *Allotments*

- *Garnishment*

A lot has changed since the days when military members were paid by officers who counted out pay in the field while using an upended drum as a table.

Most military pay now goes electronically from a finance center to a servicemember's bank. Midmonth pay periods, a comparative rarity as recently as the Vietnam War, have become routine. Here are some of the other financial programs that are important features of the military pay system.

ADVANCE PAY

It's not always possible to pay one month's bills with one month's income. This is especially true for military people who routinely face the extraordinary financial burdens of moving.

All services have provisions written into the regulations that permit the advance payment of a military paycheck. Advance pay isn't a right. Commanders can deny a request for advance pay if it appears likely to create more financial problems than it solves.

Allotments: Advance payment of Basic Pay must be organized so that military members continue their allotments for insurance and support of their dependents.

Amounts: When advance payments of Basic Pay are made, the amounts aren't the ones that appear in pay charts. Subtracted from each month's advanced Basic Pay are the following:

- Montgomery GI Bill contributions.
- Federal and state income taxes.
- Social Security taxes.
- Premiums for Servicemen's Group Life Insurance.
- Premiums for Dependent Dental Plan.
- Garnishments.
- Court-ordered support payments.
- Repayment debts to U.S. government.

Advance pay doesn't always come in a single lump-sum amount. Commanders have the authority to order payment in two or three installments.

Approval: Requests for advance pay must be approved by a servicemember's commander. In the case of recruits who request advance pay to come on active duty, that approval can be given by a recruiter.

Military folks seeking advance pay to help pay for a permanent-change-of-station (PCS) move must be able to document their projected costs.

Duration: Servicemembers in the ranks of E-1, E-2, and E-3 can receive only one month's Basic Pay in advance. Other servicemembers can receive three months' Basic Pay as advance pay.

For BAS, three months' BAS is the most that can be included in an advance payment.

Housing Advances: For military people stationed stateside, up to three months' BAQ and VHA may be advanced for unusual housing-related expenses. For people stationed overseas, one year's BAQ and OHA may be advanced.

Military members must be able to document these expenses in making a request. Regulations prohibit commanders from approving advance payment of housing allowances to purchase a home or real estate.

Repayment: Normally, advance payments of Basic Pay, BAQ, VHA, and OHA are made in 12 equal installments, beginning the month after the payment.

Recipients of advance BAS payments lose all subsequent BAS until the money has been repaid.

Servicemembers can request a faster repayment schedule. The services will require faster repayment if a servicemember is scheduled for discharge or retirement before the end of that 12-month period.

Servicemembers deployed aboard ship for more than 30 days can have their complete paychecks withheld until advance pay is repaid.

ALLOTMENTS

An allotment is an amount of money that people on active duty instruct the finance center to deduct from their regular paychecks and pay directly to someone else.

Allotments are especially useful in ensuring that financial commitments are honored when servicemembers are deployed, on sea duty, or in the field when bills become due.

Authorized Allotments: Everyone on active duty, including reservists on extended active duty, are eligible to have allotments drawn from their regular paychecks. Ineligible are reservists and

National Guardsmen officially on inactive duty and drawing Drill Pay.

The general rule is that military members can have six different allotments drawn from each military paycheck. Finance folks refer to them as discretionary allotments. But that number—six—is very misleading. Some allotments aren't counted against that limit.

The following allotments fall into the general category of payments for which you can have six:

• Payments to spouses, dependents, ex-spouses, or other family members, or to financial institutions on behalf of these people.

• Life insurance premiums.

• Deposits to banks, savings and loans, financial institutions, mutual fund companies, and investment firms.

• Mortgages or rent.

• Repayment of loans.

But there's another category of allotments that are referred to as non-discretionary. These allotments aren't counted against the six that each military member is allowed. They are:

• Delinquent federal, state or local income taxes.

• Savings bonds.

• Repayment of loans from military relief societies.

• Repayment of government debts.

• Charitable contributions to Combined Federal Campaign or military relief societies.

The military's involvement with allotments ends after the check has been written (or, more commonly, after the money has been electronically sent).

Most military members send their entire pay to a bank. If that allotment goes into a bank account that a military person jointly holds with a spouse, then the spouse doesn't need a separate allotment.

Computing Allotments: Most elements of a military paycheck can be tapped to provide an allotment. But there are limitations. Finance centers must withhold from an active-duty member's allotments enough to pay the following:

• Federal and state income taxes.
• Social Security taxes.
• Debts to the government.
• Premiums for Servicemen's Group Life Insurance.
• Deductions for the Montgomery GI Bill.

Commanders also have the authority to limit the allotments of people with chronic financial problems.

Special Circumstances: Here's how the rules for allotments affect military people and their family members in some common situations:

Death: Allotments stop at the death of the servicemember. When the recipient of an allotment dies, any uncashed allotment checks are invalid, even if received before the recipient's death.

Duration: Except in specific instances, once an allotment is started, it continues until the servicemember stops it, is discharged, or dies on active duty. Exceptions to this rule involve repaid delinquent taxes, repaid debts to the government, and contributions to service relief organizations and to the Red Cross.

Mental Incompetents: Allotments can be made to the guardians or institutions of mentally incompetent people, but not to those people directly.

Minors: Allotments can be made to the guardians or custodians of children under 16 years of age, but not directly to the minors themselves.

Power-of-Attorney: Someone with formal power-of-attorney, even a spouse, is unable to start, change, or stop allotments.

GARNISHMENT

When military members don't repay their debts, people with a claim on a military member's paycheck can take their case to the government.

The military is obligated to honor any court orders calling for the finance center to pay creditors directly from a military member's paycheck. This process is called garnishment.

Who May Garnish: Traditionally, military pay has been subject to garnishment for child support and alimony payments, settlement of debts with the government, and payment of delinquent income tax.

In 1995, private creditors—both individuals and firms—became eligible to seek court orders that call for garnishment from military paychecks.

State law in North Carolina, Pennsylvania, South Carolina, and Texas outlaw garnishment of military paychecks.

An agreement with the German government has given German courts many of the same powers to approve garnishment claims against U.S. military paychecks.

How Much: Two different formulas are used to set limits on garnishment. When garnishment is sought to settle a private or business debt, creditors are limited to a maximum of 25 percent of a military member's "disposable income."

When the garnishment is sought for child support, alimony, delinquent income taxes, or debts to the U.S. government, the finance center can send:

• Up to 50 percent of the servicemember's disposable income if the servicemember is married or supports a dependent child.

• Up to 60 percent of the servicemember's disposable income if the servicemember isn't married and doesn't have a dependent child.

• An additional penalty of 5 percent of the servicemember's disposable income if the active-duty person is at least 12 weeks behind in payments.

Calculating Limits: Again, two different systems are used for determining disposable income.

For private and business creditors, the calculation of disposable income cannot include the following:

- Exit bonuses.
- Housing allowances (BAQ, VHA, or OHA).
- Retired pay.
- Subsistence allowance (BAS).

With those exceptions, the formula for determining what a private creditor can receive 25 percent of follows the general rules listed below.

For child support, alimony, delinquent taxes, and debts to the government, most elements of a military paycheck are considered disposable income subject to garnishment. The following are *not* included:

- Basic Allowance for Quarters.
- Basic Allowance for Subsistence.
- Clothing allowances.
- Family Separation Allowance.
- Overseas Cost-of-Living Allowance.
- Overseas Housing Allowance.
- Travel allowances.
- Uniform allowances.

Finally, before allocating any money for garnishment, the finance centers make some high-priority withholdings from each military paycheck, including the following:

- Debts to U.S. government.
- Federal income tax.
- Servicemen's Group Life Insurance premiums.
- Social Security tax.
- State income tax.
- Survivor Benefit Plan premiums.

Your Rights: Servicemembers whose military pay has been targeted for garnishment have the right to notification by the military before any action is taken. They can present evidence to the finance center, especially evidence that the debt has been paid. (Remember, garnishment claims have been supported by a court order. The courts usually weed out frivolous cases.)

Military lawyers can provide advice, although they cannot represent a servicemember in court.

PART TWO

SPECIAL KINDS OF PAY

SIX

ENLISTED SIGN-UP BONUSES

In This Chapter:
- *Enlistment Bonus*
- *Reenlistment Bonus*
- *Loan Forgiveness*

If the military wants you, sometimes they'll pay to get you. All of the services have special bonuses to entice people to come on active duty or to give those already in uniform a financial reason to stay around a few years longer.

These sign-up bonuses are unique to enlisted members, although officers with highly technical skills—usually pilots and medical officers—have comparable programs, which are considered in the appropriate chapters of *Military Money Guide*. Sign-up bonuses for reservists are discussed in chapter 11, "Reserve Pays."

ENLISTMENT BONUS

The military knows that extra pay motivates people. Each

service has programs on the books that offer extra money to people who come on active duty with certain skills. The service has considerable latitude in deciding who will be offered an enlistment bonus.

Enlistment Bonus Summary:

Purpose:	To persuade people to enlist
Amount:	Maximum $12,000 (1996)
Formulas:	Vary by service, skill, commitment
Taxable:	Yes
Problem Areas:	AWOL; early release; court-martial; reservists on active duty.

Eligibility: The first step in determining eligibility for an enlistment bonus doesn't involve the new recruit. It involves the military.

Enlistment bonuses only go to people who sign formal contracts to fill crucial jobs on active duty. The military decides which skills justify the extra sign-up money.

So far as the new recruit is concerned, the following eligibility guidelines are in force:

• The new servicemember must agree to spend at least four years on active duty. (More active-duty time can be required.)

• If the recruit was a civilian who, at one time, had been on active duty for less than 180 days, that person cannot have received an enlistment bonus or a reserve bonus under the Selective Reserve Incentive Program.

• If the recruit was a civilian who, at one time, had been on active duty for at least 180 days, that person cannot have received an enlistment bonus or a reenlistment bonus for earlier service.

• If the recruit is a reservist or National Guardsman who has never before received an active-duty enlistment or reenlistment bonus, that person can qualify for an enlistment bonus. (Note: This provision concerns earlier receipt of an *active-duty* sign-up bonus, not one of the bonuses of the Selective Reserve Incentive Program.)

Rates: The maximum enlistment bonus is $12,000. The military can offer smaller amounts. Whatever the amount, it will be specified in the enlistment contract.

Payment usually begins after a new servicemember has completed training for the skill for which he or she is receiving the bonus. That skill training happens after a military person completes basic training, or boot camp.

For enlisted folks who have been in the military before and who've already undergone that skill training, the first payment comes after they've been at their first permanent assignment for at least a month.

By law, the first payment cannot be more than $7,000. The rest of the bonus will be paid in installments every three months.

Penalties: People who receive enlistment bonuses may have to repay the government for some—perhaps all—of their sign-up money if they don't complete the length of time in uniform that was agreed.

Specifically, repayment is required of people who aren't proficient in their military skill, develop disciplinary problems, or fail for other reasons to complete the full term of their enlistments.

Generally, enlisted folks discharged for medical reasons before completing their entire obligated military service can keep what they've gotten, but they aren't entitled to any unpaid portion of the bonus money.

REENLISTMENT BONUS

Selected groups of active-duty enlisted personnel are offered extra money if they agree to spend more time in the military. Because the military selects them, the bonus is called the Selective Reenlistment Bonus, or SRB.

Reenlistment Bonus Summary:

Purpose:	To persuade people to stay in uniform
Amount:	Maximum $45,000 (1996)
Formulas:	Vary by service, skill, commitment
Taxable:	Yes
Problem Area:	Early release

Eligibility: The first step in deciding eligibility for a reenlistment bonus involves the military, not the servicemember.

Reenlistment bonuses go only to people possessing skills that the military says it will pay extra to hold on to.

Even then, not everyone with that skill can receive a reenlistment bonus. Military regulations break down a military career into three zones. Slightly different eligibility rules affect each zone.

Zone A: To be eligible, people must have at least 21 months of continuous active duty but less than six years and must reenlist for at least three years. At the end of that enlistment, they must have at least six years on active duty. Also, they must not have received a Zone A reenlistment bonus before.

Zone B: To be eligible, servicemembers must have at least six years on active duty, but less than 10 years, and must reenlist for at least three years. At the end of that enlistment, they must have at least 10 years on active duty. They must not have received a Zone B reenlistment bonus before.

Zone C: To be eligible, people must have at least 10 years on active duty but less than 14 years, and must reenlist for at least three years. At the end of that enlistment they must have at least 14 years on active duty. They must not have received a Zone C reenlistment bonus before.

Each service identifies the skills for which it's willing to pay reenlistment bonuses, and the amount of experience—or "zone"—where it may encounter staffing problems.

Rates: The maximum reenlistment bonus that servicemembers can receive for committing themselves to another stretch on active duty is $45,000.

How much an individual military person will be paid relies upon a three-step formula:

- Determine a military person's monthly Basic Pay.
- Multiply that by a special figure—called a multiple—that the government offers for reenlisting. The maximum multiple is 10.
- Multiply that figure by the number of years for which the servicemember is reenlisting.

Some of the finer points about that formula can be very important for large numbers of military people.

For example, if you still have time remaining on one enlistment contract when you reenlist, that remaining time will be subtracted from the amount of time credited as the length of your reenlistment.

Payments are made by a combination of the lump-sum and annual methods. Servicemembers should learn the exact schedule for their payments before they sign the reenlistment contract. Up to half of the total reenlistment bonus can be paid immediately, usually upon the first day of a servicemember's new enlistment. The rest is divided into equal segments and paid on the anniversary of the first payment.

Payments aren't made after 16 years of time in service. Someone reenlisting with a bonus and with 13 years in uniform will be allowed to receive the bonus only for 3 years of additional service, although the actual enlistment may be longer.

Penalties: People who receive reenlistment bonuses may have to repay the government for some—perhaps all—of their sign-up money if they don't complete the length of time in uniform that was called for in their reenlistment contracts.

Specifically, repayment is required of people who aren't proficient in their military skill, develop disciplinary problems with the military, lose a security clearance necessary for doing their job, or fail for other reasons to complete the full length of their commitments.

Generally, enlisted folks discharged for medical reasons before completing their entire obligated military service can keep what they've gotten, but they aren't entitled to any unpaid portion of the bonus money.

Special Circumstances: Here's how the regulations for reenlistment bonuses apply to specific situations.

Broken Service: Reenlistment bonuses can go to some people who are civilians when they sign their reenlistment contracts. These are former enlisted people who reenlist within three months after being discharged.

Pay Raise: The exact size of a reenlistment bonus is determined by a formula that includes a servicemember's Basic Pay, but it's not recalculated whenever a military person receives a pay raise.

Prior-Service Officers: Generally, people who have been officers are ineligible to receive reenlistment bonuses if they come back on active duty as enlisted people.

An exception involves a narrowly defined group of former officers. They can qualify for a reenlistment bonus if they meet both of the following conditions:

• They were active-duty enlisted before they became officers.

• They reenlisted within three months after being discharged as officers.

For them, the reenlistment bonus could apply to their first stint on active duty after losing their commissions, so long as they otherwise qualify.

LOAN FORGIVENESS

The most direct way to keep money in your wallet is to not spend it. The military has a sign-up bonus that does exactly that. The military can forgive some federally-backed student loans for enlisted members who agree to spend certain amounts of time in uniform.

Loan Forgiveness Program Summary:	
Purpose:	To repay student loans in return for service
Formula:	One-third of loan or $1,500 yearly
Amount:	Varies
Taxable:	No
Loophole:	No repayment for early release.

This loan-forgiveness program, which shows up in federal law as the "Educational Loan Repayment Program," isn't guaranteed to anyone. It's a management tool that the military can use to solve certain staffing shortfalls.

Eligibility: Three general rules determine who can qualify. Eligible people are:

• Enlisted.

• In skills areas officially deemed "critical" by military.

• Holding certain federally backed student loans.

Technically, those loans are made, insured, or guaranteed under parts B and E of the Higher Education Act of 1965.

Rates: There are two simple formulas for determining how much of a total student debt will be forgiven each year for participants. Eligible enlisted members are covered by the formula that produces the larger figure.

Specifically, participants can be forgiven for one-third of the debt or $1,500, whichever is larger.

Interest continues to accumulate until a loan is completely paid off. Participants don't have to repay the government for any part of the forgiven debt if they leave active duty.

SEVEN

HAZARDOUS DUTY PAYS

Military life is surrounded by risks. Normal on-the-job experiences include proximity to heavy equipment, explosives, and dangerous substances like jet fuel and chemical propellants. The ultimate risk, of course, is combat.

Congress and the Pentagon have established special kinds of pay that reward people financially for the jobs that they do. This extra money is more a token payment than a true reflection of the value of the job being done.

HOSTILE FIRE/IMMINENT DANGER PAY

It used to be called combat pay. The name has been changed—now it can be called Hostile Fire Pay or Imminent Danger Pay—but it still is financial recognition of dangers of being close to shots fired in anger.

Hostile Fire/Imminent Danger Pay Summary:	
Purpose:	Financial recognition for extra risks
Amounts:	$150 monthly (1996)
Formula:	None, same rate for officers and enlisted
Taxable:	Generally, yes
Loopholes:	Qualifying for one day results in full month's payment
Problem Area:	Combat zone exclusion

Hostile Fire Pay and Imminent Danger Pay are the very same thing. For simplicity's sake, unless clearly noted otherwise, everything said here about Hostile Fire Pay applies to Imminent Danger Pay.

Eligibility: There are two basic methods—geographic and individual—to determine eligibility for Hostile Fire Pay.

For early 1996, service in one of 21 areas qualified military folks for Hostile Fire Pay:

- In Europe: countries of the former Yugoslavia.
- In the Middle East: Iran, Iraq, Kuwait, Lebanon, Turkey, airspace above the Middle East.
- In Southeast Asia: Cambodia, Laos, Vietnam.
- In South and Central America: Columbia, El Salvador, Peru.
- In Africa: Angola, Chad, Liberia, Mozambique, Somalia.
- In Asia: Afghanistan.

There is also a second, case-by-case route to eligibility:

• A member of the U.S. military is killed, wounded, or injured by hostile fire, by the explosion of a hostile mine or by hostile action.

• A member of the U.S. military is subjected to hostile fire, explosions, or mines.

This case-by-case eligibility for Hostile Fire Pay is usually done in terms of naval vessels, aircraft, and the smallest ground unit in the vicinity of hostile fire. If anyone on a vessel or aircraft or in a ground unit becomes eligible for this extra pay, everyone does.

Rates: Hostile Fire Pay is $150 per month (1996) for all eligible personnel.

The servicemember who's been in the combat zone for a complete month and the person who arrives on the last day of the month both receive a full month's rate of $150.

You can receive only one month's Hostile Fire Pay for any calendar month.

Taxes: Hostile Fire Pay and Imminent Danger Pay are usually taxable.

They are protected from income taxes only when earned in a geographic area especially designated by the president as a tax-free zone. (See chapter 4, "Taxes.") Few geographic zones set up for Hostile Fire Pay are also tax-free zones.

Special Cases: Here's how the fine print in the rules for Hostile Fire Pay and Imminent Danger Pay affect specific groups of servicemembers:

AWOL: Military people who lose all pay and allowances for having left their units without permission also lose Hostile Fire and Imminent Danger Pay for the duration of their absences.

Court-Martial: Military people convicted by a court-martial and sentenced to the loss of all pay also lose their Hostile Fire and Imminent Danger Pay computed to a daily rate.

Death: The survivors of people who die in a geographic area designated for Hostile Fire or Imminent Danger Pay are paid the extra money computed on a daily basis. If the deceased servicemember qualified using the case-by-case method discussed above, the payment is made for the entire last month of the military person's life.

Hospitalization: Military personnel hospitalized in a combat zone with wounds or injuries received while eligible for Hostile Fire or Imminent Danger Pay continue to get the extra money. Payments stop after three months for those hospitalized outside the geographic area designated for this pay.

Leave: Taking leave during a month for which you're eligible for Hostile Fire or Imminent Danger Pay doesn't affect either your eligibility or the amount of extra pay you'll receive.

A military person assigned outside a combat zone can't qualify on leave by traveling into a geographic area designated for Hostile Fire or Imminent Danger Pay.

HAZARDOUS DUTY PAY BASICS

With the exception of Hostile Fire Pay and Imminent Danger Pay, the other kinds of hazardous duty pay mentioned in this chapter share many of the same rules. They're officially lumped together as Hazardous Duty Incentive Pays (HDIPs).

To save space and eliminate some repetition, we'll discuss the general rules that apply to all of them. Then, we'll consider the specific rules peculiar to each one.

Eligibility: Hazardous duty pay is available to all members of the military who also meet specific eligibility criteria.

In most cases, recipients must perform the hazardous work as part of their official, full-time duties.

Rates: With one exception, the rate for hazardous duty pay is $110 per month (1996) for all military members.

The only people who receive more are parachutists who regularly jump at extremely high altitudes and open their chutes at extremely low altitudes. They can qualify for an extra $165 monthly (1996).

This extra money is paid day-by-day, not month-by-month. For periods of eligibility less than an entire month, military folks receive a daily rate of $3.67.

Military personnel can receive only two of the hazardous duty pays mentioned below, plus Hostile Fire or Imminent Danger Pay.

Reserves: Members of the reserves and the National Guard are eligible to receive all of the hazardous duty pays while on active duty.

During drill periods, which are officially known as inactive duty for training, they can receive only Demolition Pay, Experimental Stress Pay, Flight Deck Pay, and Parachute Duty Pay.

Special Circumstances: Certain special categories of military personnel are subject to special treatment in the regulations.

Illness: Recipients of hazardous duty pay who are unable to perform their military jobs because of illness continue to receive the extra money in their paychecks.

Injury: Military members injured by the thing or activity that's hazardous are usually eligible to receive the extra money for three months.

People receiving two different kinds of hazardous duty pay who are injured by the thing or activity that's hazardous and who become unable to continue their duties are usually eligible to receive both kinds of hazardous duty pay for three months.

When the injury wasn't caused by the hazardous duty, recipients lose the extra money when they're unable to perform those duties.

Leave: Recipients of hazardous duty pay who are on leave continue to receive the extra money.

POW or MIA: Military personnel who were receiving one of the hazardous duty pays when they became prisoners of war, missing in action, or placed officially on "missing status" continue to receive the extra money for the duration of their absence.

Folks who return to U.S. control continue to receive hazardous duty pay for up to a year.

Temporary Duty: Recipients on temporary duty or temporary additional duty continue to receive the extra money in their paychecks.

CHEMICAL MUNITIONS PAY

Recipients of Chemical Munitions Pay must be in military jobs whose primary tasks involve, according to the regulations, "the direct physical handling" of chemical munitions.

This "handling" can involve the storage, maintenance, testing, assembly, disassembly, disposal, or transportation of chemical weapons.

Kinds of service that *do not* qualify military folks for this addition to their paychecks are the following:

• Working with riot-control gas, defoliants, or smoke-producing or flame-producing materials.

• Loading shells or bombs containing chemical munitions into artillery tubes, aircraft, or other delivery systems.

• Being in contact with chemical weapons during storage in the field.

• Handling individual components of so-called binary weapons.

• Conducting laboratory tests upon the materials used in chemical munitions.

When in doubt about eligibility, officials return to the basics. Chemical Munitions Pay was designed for members of the armed forces whose official duties made them vulnerable to the accidental exposure to chemical agents. It's not for military folks who've been around these dangerous weapons.

DANGEROUS ORGANISMS PAY

Recipients of Dangerous Organisms Pay have been assigned for at least 30 consecutive days to a laboratory in which their primary duty involves working with certain organisms. The work must involve organisms that are deadly and for which no form of immunization is available.

Dangerous Organisms Pay goes to people with direct, immediate, constant exposure from handling these deadly materials. Working in the vicinity of these viruses and bacteria won't qualify anyone for extra money.

DEMOLITION DUTY PAY

Military members eligible for Demolition Duty Pay have, as their "primary duty," to quote the regulations, the use of high explosives.

The regulations mention four specific categories of military jobs that make people eligible for Demolition Duty Pay, all sharing the requirement that military members work full time with explosives:

- Using explosives to demolish objects, obstacles, or other explosives.
- Disarming explosives.
- Serving as instructors in the use of demolitions, provided that the instruction include the use of live explosives.
- Overseeing proficiency training for other demolitions workers, again provided that live explosives are used.

Folks in training to become explosives experts are singled out in the regulations as being eligible for the Demolition Duty Pay, even though they haven't taken up their full-time duties.

DIVING PAY

Each service has divers, but each service calls upon them to do different things. Consequently, Diving Pay doesn't come with a one-size-fits-all rule book.

Generally, enlisted members and officers of the Army, Navy, and Marine Corps who are attending diving school become eligible for Diving Pay on the date of their first dive. Eligibility ends on the day they are dropped from the course or they graduate. For those assigned to diving duty, eligibility resumes when they're put on orders for duty as divers.

In the Air Force, both officers and enlisted members receive Diving Pay when assigned to diving duty. They don't qualify for the extra money while training to become divers.

The minimum Diving Pay is $110 per month. Officers are limited to a maximum payment of $200 monthly (although only a few diving-qualified officers receive the maximum).

The top enlisted rate is $300 monthly, again with only a handful of each service's top enlisted divers receiving the maximum.

Rates: Here's a summary of the highlights on rates, using 1995 statistics for each service.

Army: Officers receive $110 monthly during training, then $175 monthly for combat divers and $200 for marine diving officers. Enlisted divers receive $110 monthly during training, then $110 monthly for second-class divers, $135 for salvage divers, $175 monthly for first-class divers and combat divers, and $300 monthly for master divers.

Navy: Officers receive $110 monthly during training, then $110 monthly for diving officers (scuba) and some SEALs, and $200 monthly for other categories of eligible officers. Navy enlisted members receive $110 monthly during training, then up to $300 monthly, depending on skill level and assignment, with the maximum rates going to master divers and some SEAL delivery vehicle pilots and navigators.

Air Force: Neither officers nor enlisted members receive Diving Pay during training. Qualified officers receive $150 monthly after assignment. Enlisted members who are scuba divers draw $110 monthly, while pararescue divers receive $150 monthly.

Marine Corps: Officers receive $110 monthly during training, then $150 monthly if assigned to duty requiring the use of scuba equipment. Enlisted members receive $110 monthly during training and during their assignment to full-time diving duties.

Special Circumstances: A variety of special circumstances can affect a servicemember's eligibility for diving pay. Here are some of the most common problems.

Court-Martial: Recipients of Diving Pay who are confined awaiting court-martial have the extra money suspended. If acquitted, they receive full Diving Pay, including money for the period of their confinement.

Hospitalization: Divers who are hospitalized because of a diving accident can continue receiving Diving Pay for 90 days. If the hospitalization was unrelated to diving, Diving Pay continues for 30 days.

Lapsed Qualification: Divers who lose their technical qualifications to dive are ineligible to receive Diving Pay, even if they're diving during the period of lapsed qualification. If they regain their qualifications and regain Diving Pay, they cannot be paid for the period their qualification lapsed.

Leave: Recipients of Diving Pay continue to receive it for 30 days while on leave.

Temporary Duty: Divers who are on temporary duty unrelated to diving can receive Diving Pay only for the first 30 days of their temporary-duty assignment.

Split Hairs: Technically, Diving Pay isn't classified as a hazardous duty pay. It's been placed in this section because that's where many folks expect it to be.

An important trait of Diving Pay involves multiple eligibility for hazardous duty pay. Recipients of Diving Pay can receive Hostile Fire or Imminent Danger Pay, plus only one of the other hazardous duty pays.

EXPERIMENTAL STRESS PAY

Experimental Stress Pay doesn't go to everyone in the military who's been subjected to harsh physical conditions.

Recipients have performed one of the following kinds of duty within a calendar month:

• Personnel who are research subjects in acceleration or deceleration experiments.

• Military people who are research subjects in so-called thermal experiments involving extremes of heat or cold.

• Personnel who serve inside high-pressure or low-pressure chambers as research subjects, technicians monitoring or servicing equipment, or instructors.

This last category applies to many Navy personnel who use high-pressure chambers to train and to give medical care to deep-sea divers. The Navy's rules have further restrictions and requirements for so-called instructor-observers.

PARACHUTE PAY

Recipients of Parachute Pay, both the regular rate and the HALO rate, are under orders to serve as parachutists or parachute riggers.

Additionally, they must actually bail out of aircraft a minimum number of times during a fixed period. Generally, they must jump once every three months.

Recipients of the HALO (High Altitude, Low Opening) rate must have undergone training in free-fall operations from a course that's either run by the military or officially recognized as meeting the military's training standards for HALO operations. They must also must meet the one-jump-in-three-months rule.

Some military parachutists find themselves alternating between the regular rate and the HALO rate, depending on their jump schedules. That's okay.

Rate: Normally, Parachute Pay is paid at a monthly rate. That's $110 monthly at the regular rate and $165 at the HALO rate.

Parachutists who qualify for both rates in a calendar month receive the higher HALO rate.

Three-Month Rule: Normally, a parachute jump qualifies the servicemember for Parachute Pay during the month of the jump, the calendar month before the jump, and the calendar month after the jump.

If it's advantageous to the servicemember, a single jump can qualify a person for Parachute Pay during the month of the jump and the two calendar months before the jump, or for the month of the jump and the two calendar months after the jump.

The three-month rule can be waived by commanders when military personnel are unable to jump because they're engaged in combat operations.

The three-month rule can also be altered, somewhat, when certain factors other than combat keep a parachutist from jumping. Specifically, military jumpers can qualify for 12 months of Parachute Pay by making one jump during a three-month period, followed by three other jumps at any time during the next nine months.

This 12-month qualification is limited to parachutists who are prevented from keeping up with their usual cycle of jumps because of military operations affecting their entire unit, or the absence of the equipment needed to jump or the absence of an aircraft.

Nonqualifying Jumps: Specifically *not* qualifying for Parachute Pay are jumps made on leave, on temporary duty to an assignment not requiring parachute jumps, or by reservists on active duty in assignments not requiring parachute jumps.

TOXIC FUELS PAY

Military personnel who have, as their "primary duty," according to the regulations, the handling of some specific, unusually dangerous fuels are entitled to extra money in their monthly military paychecks.

The fuels include:

- H-70.
- Inhibited red-fuming nitric acid.
- JP-X.
- Liquid oxidizer-nitrogen tetroxide.
- Unsymmetrical dimethyl hydrazine.

The services have the authority to identify other kinds of toxic fuels that will qualify military personnel for Toxic Fuels Pay.

As with some of the other hazardous duty pays, just being around the thing that makes a military job officially "hazardous" isn't enough to qualify someone for the extra money. This pay program was set up to compensate folks who work with these dangerous materials up close, every day.

TOXIC PESTICIDES PAY

Recipients of Toxic Pesticides Pay generally are assigned to military units or offices involved with entomology, pest control, pest management, or preventative medicine.

Recipients must be assigned to that organization for at least 30 consecutive days, being subject to frequent and regular exposure to certain highly toxic pesticides used in fumigation.

If there's no fumigation performed by a servicemember during a month, there's no Toxic Pesticides Pay in the paycheck.

Among the chemicals specifically mentioned in the regulations that qualify military personnel for this extra money are phosphine, sulfuryl fluoride, hydrogen cyanide, and methyl bromide. The services can add others.

All of these qualifying chemicals are used in fumigation. Solid chemicals used outdoors against burrowing animals are specifically cited in the regulations for *not* making military personnel eligible for Toxic Pesticides Pay.

EIGHT

SPECIAL SKILLS PAYS

In This Chapter:
- *Special Duty*
  Assignment Pay
- *Foreign Language Pay*

- *Engineering and*
  Scientific Pay

Not all military jobs are equal. Some require finely tuned skills that are difficult to acquire and tough to maintain. Finding and keeping enough people with those skills can be a difficult task for the military's personnel specialists.

This chapter will consider the basic rules governing some programs for people with special skills. Other kinds of payments can be found in appropriately named chapters, such as "Flight Pays" and "Naval Pays."

The term *Special Skills Pays* isn't one that's recognized by the military. Strolling into a military pay office and asking for the latest details about Special Skills Pays will only bring puzzled looks. The phrase is used here because it's useful.

SPECIAL DUTY ASSIGNMENT PAY

About 50,000 active-duty people have skills that their services have decided are worth extra money. The additional income takes the form of Special Duty Assignment Pay.

Like many extra kinds of military compensation, payment of Special Duty Assignment Pay is driven by the military. It's there to fill necessary jobs with the proper people. It's not a financial right.

Special Duty Assignment Pay Summary:	
Purpose:	Extra money for needed skills
Rates:	$55 to $275 monthly (1996)
Formula:	By skill level
Taxable:	Yes
Problem Areas:	Annual certification, only for enlisted personnel

Some folks still refer to this payment as Proficiency Pay or Pro Pay. That's the name of a similar program that closed in 1984.

Eligibility: Special Duty Assignment Pay is for enlisted members only. Recipients must be on active duty in the rank of E-3 or in a higher rank. They also must possess a skill for which their branch of the military is willing to pay extra money.

The services have great freedom in deciding which skills merit extra money in the paycheck. The general rule is that the assignments must be unusually difficult or they must demand a high level of responsibility.

Once a military skill has been identified, everyone who fits into that group on the basis of MOS, AFS, rating, career field, or occupational field is entitled to this supplemental pay.

The process also works in reverse. If recipients lose the

technical proficiency for which they're being paid, they also lose the extra money.

Eligibility for Special Duty Assignment Pay isn't affected by any other kind of pay or allowance. Nor does it, in turn, limit eligibility for any other kind of military compensation.

Rates: Payments for Special Duty Assignment Pay are made monthly, as part of a regular military paycheck.

There are five possible amounts. How much a given service-member will receive is determined by the rules of the parent service. Service regulations not only identify qualifying skills for Special Duty Assignment Pay, but also place each skill into one of these five levels.

Each skill level has its own monthly rate. Here are the rates in effect for 1996:

SD-1	$55
SD-2	110
SD-3	165
SD-4	220
SD-5	275

These rates aren't the kind that change every year to keep up with the rise in inflation. In fact, they tend to stay as they are for many years.

Reservists: Reservists and National Guardsmen on drill status are ineligible for Special Duty Assignment Pay.

Generally, reservists who otherwise qualify for Special Duty Assignment Pay can receive the extra money while on active duty.

The major group of active-duty reservists and active-duty National Guardsmen who are *not* eligible for this extra payment are those who are on active duty for training for periods less than 180 days.

Special Circumstances: Like most programs that put extra money into a military paycheck, a variety of situations can affect eligibility for the extra money. Here are some of the more common special cases:

AWOL: Special Duty Assignment Pay isn't paid when recipients are officially classified as absent without leave.

Confinement: Recipients lose this extra money if confined because of a court-martial sentence or as a result of nonjudicial punishment—that is, Article 15 or Captain's Mast. The extra payment resumes at the end of the confinement, so long as the servicemember still meets eligibility standards.

Hospitalization: Generally, military folks who are unable to perform the duty for which they were paid Special Duty Assignment Pay continue to receive the pay while hospitalized or on convalescent leave.

Payments can last for 12 months during hospitalization.

Folks with medical problems that render them incapable of performing that special extra duty become ineligible for this extra money after they leave the hospital or return to duty.

If the cause of the hospitalization or convalescent leave was related to alcoholism or drug abuse, then Special Duty Assignment Pay stops until the servicemember is fit for work again.

Leave: Recipients of this extra money can continue receiving it while on authorized leave.

Temporary Duty: What happens to recipients of special duty assignment pay while on temporary duty depends upon that duty.

If the temporary duty requires the use of the skill for which the military member is receiving the extra pay, then it continues throughout the period of temporary duty.

If the temporary duty doesn't require the use of those special skills, then Special Duty Assignment Pay ends on the 91st day of temporary duty.

Training: Since this extra money is related to proficiency in on-the-job skills, a complicated set of rules applies whenever recipients take part in formal training programs. Generally, the rules fall into three categories.

First, if the training is related to the special skill, then the special duty assignment pay continues throughout the training.

Second, if the training is *not* related to the special skill but the military member will be returning to an assignment using that skill when the course ends, then the extra pay can continue for 90 days.

Third, if the training isn't related to the special skill and the military member won't be returning to an assignment using that skill after completion of the class, then special duty assignment pay ends when the military member leaves his or her unit to attend the training.

FOREIGN LANGUAGE PAY

Intelligence operations have always relied upon understanding potential enemies, and that understanding begins at a very basic level. We must understand what they are saying.

Foreign Language Pay Summary:	
Purpose:	Incentive for learning targeted languages
Rates:	$25 to $100 monthly (1996)
Formula:	By skill level
Taxable:	Generally, yes. Not for Social Security
Problem Areas:	Annual certification.

Since 1987, a program has been on the books to encourage military members to learn, retain, and improve their language skills. Officially called Foreign Language *Proficiency* Pay, it's commonly called simply Foreign Language Pay.

Eligibility: Technically, Foreign Language Pay is open to officers and enlisted members, both on active duty and in the reserve components.

It doesn't go to everyone who knows a foreign language, however, nor even to extremely fluent students of a language. The first rule of eligibility is that the military picks the languages for which it's willing to pay extra money.

Recipients must pass through an unusually large number of eligibility "hoops," including these:

• Their military skill requires language proficiency.

• The job they're assigned to requires language proficiency.

• They know a language for which the military has authorized the extra pay.

• They've undergone language training recognized by the Department of Defense.

• They meet and maintain proficiency standards set up by the military, including an annual certification.

This is a fairly complex set of requirements. If you fail to meet any one of them, odds are you won't get—or keep—the additional money in your military paycheck.

Rates: Payments for Foreign Language Pay are made monthly, as part of a regular military paycheck.

There are four possible amounts. How much a given servicemember will receive is determined by the rules of the parent service. Generally, the more proficient the service member and the more important that proficiency is to the military, the larger the payment.

Each skill level has its own monthly rate. Here are the rates in effect for 1996:

FLPP-1	$ 25
FLPP-2	50
FLPP-3	75
FLPP-4	100

These rates aren't the kind that change every year to keep up with the rise in inflation. In fact, the rates in effect in 1996 were the same ones in effect when Congress first created this program in 1986.

Reserves: Members of the reserves and National Guard who are on active duty can qualify for Foreign Language Pay, just like anyone else in uniform.

And, breaking a general pattern, this is one kind of extra payment that also can go to members of the reserves and National Guard on inactive duty for training, as the regular weekend drill periods are technically called.

Eligible reservists receive one-thirtieth of the monthly rate, appropriate for their skill level, for each drill period that they serve. Since a typical two-day weekend has four drill periods, then recipients would receive four-thirtieths of the monthly rate each month.

Reservists are also eligible for the daily rate of Foreign Language Pay for other kinds of reserve-related assignments, including training.

ENGINEERING AND SCIENTIFIC PAY

When no other inducement is available to persuade scientists and engineers to spend some time in uniform, the services can offer them a bonus for obtaining and retaining their technical skills and for staying in the military.

Engineering and Scientific Pay Summary:	
Purpose:	Incentive to stay after initial tour
Rates:	Up to $3,000 annually (1996)
Formula:	Individually set
Taxable:	Yes
Problem Areas:	Needs of the service, discharge.

Officially called Engineering and Scientific Career Continuation Pay, it's a very narrowly drawn program, used by the services to meet manpower needs when nothing else will do the trick.

Eligibility: Engineering and Scientific Pay is available only to commissioned officers on active duty. It's not open to warrant officers, nor to enlisted members or members of the reserves or National Guard.

The most important eligibility rule involves the needs of the service. Even if people fully meet all of the criteria to qualify for this bonus, they still cannot get it unless the parent service decides that it needs folks badly enough to pay extra money for it.

With that in mind, recipients must also meet a number of other eligibility requirements. They must:

• Hold a degree in engineering or science from an accredited college or university;.

• Be in the rank O-6 or at a lower rank.

• Have duties as an engineer or scientist.

• Have at least 3 years in the military but not more than 19 years.

• Be assigned to duties that the parent service has selected for payment of this bonus.

• Meet the military's rules for technical expertise in an engineering or scientific field.

Someone meeting all these formal eligibility rules must agree in writing to spend at least another year on active duty in a key engineering or scientific field. One year is the minimum, four years the maximum.

Officers who are on drill status with the reserves or National Guard, performing regular weekend drills, cannot qualify for this extra pay.

Rates: The maximum payment under this program is $3,000 per year for each additional year in uniform. The services have the discretion to offer smaller amounts.

The services also have latitude in deciding how it will be paid—as lump-sum yearly bonuses, as quarterly payments, or as regular portions of the monthly paycheck.

Penalties: Because the military people receiving this extra pay are in high demand by the civilian world, the regulations are unusually specific about what to do if recipients don't complete the full period of service they've committed themselves to perform.

Generally, if military members are paid a full year's bonus and don't serve that year on active duty, they must repay the bonus for the unserved time.

Declaring personal bankruptcy won't get you off the hook for making repayments.

Offering to repay the unserved portion of the bonus if the military cancels the contract won't release you from active duty.

Recipients who lose the technical proficiency for which they've been paid the bonus are treated the same as people with unserved time. They must repay the government the bonus money for time after they lost their proficiency.

A few categories of recipients can retain the extra money even if they don't serve all of the time for which they're committed. This includes people with medical disabilities and those discharged early through no fault of their own.

NINE

FLIGHT PAYS

The armed forces offer extra money to military people for three basic reasons: because they do things that are dangerous, because they have skills that are technically demanding, and because they have skills that are wanted by the private sector.

When it comes to flying, all three reasons come into play. To ensure that the military has enough men and women to fulfill its missions in the air, and to guarantee the right mix of skills and time in service, the military offers an array of annual bonuses and one-time payments to its flight crews.

FLIGHT PAY (ACIP)

For nearly as long as there have been airplanes that belonged to the U.S. military, there have been financial incentives that over the years have had many names. For most people, however, it was simply "Flight Pay."

ACIP Summary:	
Purpose:	Financial recognition of skills, incentive to stay
Amounts:	$1,500 to $7,800 annually (1996)
Formula:	By service, aircraft, length of commitment
Taxable:	Yes

Since 1974, Flight Pay has been more technically known as Aviation Career Incentive Pay (ACIP). Generally, it's restricted to people whose jobs are in the cockpit of an aircraft. Other crewmembers and other servicemembers whose duties require regular time in an aircraft have their own versions of flight pay, which are discussed below.

Eligibility: Usually, aviators are eligible for ACIP if they spend at least four hours each calendar month in flight, which is defined as the time between takeoff and coming to a complete stop after landing. Month-to-month eligibility is called conditional ACIP.

Anyone who hasn't flown in a given month can use the flight hours accumulated during the five previous calendar months. The same hour of flight can be used only once.

Commanding officers can certify that officers were unable to meet these minimal time-in-flight requirements because of military operations, combat, or the unavailability of aircraft. With that certification, an officer has six consecutive months to accumulate 24 flight hours.

"Continuous" Eligibility: Aviators with a fixed amount of time in the cockpit are guaranteed ACIP until they reach certain points in their careers.

To qualify, they must meet certain standards. Flight crews refer to them as "gates." The rules governing gates measure time as "aviation service," which is the period since entering flight school. Those standards are as follows:

• *Six years of flight duty within 12 years after entering flight school:* Guaranteed continual monthly ACIP until the end of the 18th year of aviation service.

• *At least nine years, but less than 11 years, of flight duty within 18 years after entering flight school:* Guaranteed continual monthly ACIP until end of 22nd year of aviation service.

• *At least 11 years of actual flight duty within 18 years after entering flight school:* Guaranteed continual monthly ACIP until end of 25th year of aviation service.

All continual monthly ACIP ends after 25 years. Officers who fail to pass through one of these eligibility hoops don't receive guaranteed monthly ACIP payments, but they are entitled to receive flight pay for any month in which they're flying for the military. This also applies to officers past the 25-year mark.

Rates: ACIP has two fundamentally different formulas that are used to compute rates.

People begin receiving flight pay based upon the number of years of their aviation service. This ACIP formula is called Phase One by the military:

Years of Flying	Monthly Rate
2 or less	$125
Over 2	156
Over 3	188
Over 4	206
Over 6	650

ACIP for warrant officers is always based upon this Phase One formula. And most commissioned officers receive their ACIP under the maximum category—"over 6"—for most of their careers.

However, when a commissioned officer reaches the 18th anniversary of entering the military, the ACIP formula changes. No longer is it based upon years as a flier, but years spent as a military officer.

The second ACIP formula, called Phase Two, looks like this:

Years as Officer	Monthly Rate
Over 18	$585
Over 20	495
Over 22	385
Over 25	250

An officer with more than 18 years' commissioned time but less than six years' aviation time is entitled to the more generous, aviation-based ACIP of Phase One.

Restrictions are placed on generals and admirals who qualify for ACIP payments. O-7s cannot receive more than $200 monthly in ACIP money, while O-8s, O-9s, and O-10s cannot be paid more than $206 monthly.

Special Circumstances: Here are some of the finer points about ACIP and its application to officers in very specific situations:

Crewmembers, Non-Crewmembers Pay: Recipients of ACIP, both the continuous and the conditional varieties, are ineligible for any other kind of flight pay, such as the ones discussed below for crewmembers and non-crewmembers.

Flight Surgeons: Medical officers and flight surgeons who are required to fly qualify for Conditional ACIP. Like everyone else in that category, they must meet minimum time-in-flight requirements each month to receive the extra money.

Injury: Generally, an officer receiving continuous ACIP payments who becomes unable to meet the medical standards to fly, whether the injury was flight-related or not, continues to receive ACIP monthly payments for 180 days.

An officer receiving Conditional ACIP continues to receive

the extra income for three months following a flight-related injury. If the injury isn't flight related, the officer must meet the usual standards of four flight-hours per month.

Missing: ACIP recipients who become missing in action are eligible for the extra money during the entire period of their absence, plus a maximum of one year after their return.

Reserves: Reservists on inactive-duty status, as the weekend drills are officially called, can receive monthly ACIP payments. They must fly two hours during a calendar month.

Suspension: An officer declared "disqualified for aviation service" for any reason—except medical problems—immediately loses the right to ACIP payments, effective the day of the disqualification.

MIDCAREER AVIATION BONUS

One of the toughest times for the military to hold on to valuable people is during midcareer. That's when the initial enthusiasm of being in uniform has worn off but the lure of a military retirement is too distant to exert much influence.

Midcareer Aviation Bonus Summary:	
Purpose:	Incentive for fliers to commit to one more year
Amounts:	$6,000 to $12,000 annually (1996)
Rates:	By service, aircraft, length of commitment
Taxable:	Yes
Loopholes:	Can pick formula, add-on to flight pay
Problem Areas:	Heavily controlled by services.

To counter the midcareer doldrums, the Pentagon offers the Aviator Retention Bonus, which is also known as Aviator Continuation Pay. Who gets it and how much they get vary by service.

Eligibility: The Aviator Retention Bonus is governed by two layers of eligibility rules. The first, most basic rules are set by Congress and the Defense Department. They stipulate that recipients must:

- Be qualified by the military for "operational flying duty."
- Be no higher than O-5 in rank.
- Have completed initial active-duty commitment for undergraduate aviator training.
- Have completed at least six years of active duty.
- Not have completed 13 years of active duty.

Note that the rules that mention time in the military define it as total time on active duty, not years on flight status.

The second set of rules is made by the individual services. The services' rules cannot be more generous than DoD's rules, but they can—and often are—less generous.

Bonus recipients are also eligible for ACIP flight pay.

Rates: The Aviator Bonus comes in two versions. There's a smaller bonus for people who make short-term extensions of their military commitments and a larger bonus for people who make long-term commitments.

Short-term Bonus: A maximum of $6,000 annually for officers who agree to extend their military obligations by one or two years.

Long-term Bonus: A maximum of $12,000 annually. It goes to officers who extend their military commitments however long it takes to reach 14 years of service.

If an officer is eligible for both at the same time, that person gets the more generous long-term bonus.

Any officer who receives a bonus and fails to serve the full term of the commitment must repay the government for the unserved portion of the bonus.

Service Restrictions: The individual services have wide authority to award the Aviator Bonus in ways that solve that service's manpower problems.

Here's how the services shaped their own eligibility rules for the Aviator Bonus in 1996:

Army: Not given to anyone.

Navy: Long-term bonuses given to crewmembers of specific aircraft; some rates less than the maximums. No short-term bonuses offered.

Air Force: Long-term bonuses available to all air-crew members with seven years' service. Must meet other eligibility rules. Short-term bonuses for shorter commitments.

Marine Corps: Short-term bonuses given to crew members of specific aircraft. No long-term bonuses given.

Coast Guard: Not given to anyone.

CREWMEMBERS FLIGHT PAY

Not everyone assigned to fly aboard a military aircraft is a pilot, co-pilot, or navigator receiving Flight Pay, or Aviation Career Incentive Pay, (ACIP), as it's now technically known.

Crewmembers Flight Pay Summary:	
Purpose:	Financial recognition of extra hazards
Amounts:	$110 to $250 monthly (1996)
Rates:	By rank only
Taxable:	Yes
Problem Areas:	Not paid with any other form of flight pay.

Other people assigned to the crew of a military aircraft are also eligible for their own version of Flight Pay. Technically, it's called Hazardous Duty Incentive Pay for Flying Duty. It doesn't go to people who are eligible for ACIP or the flight pay given to AWACS crews.

Eligibility: Active-duty personnel are eligible for extra money if their official duties require "regular and frequent aerial flights as crew." Primarily, this extra pay goes to enlisted members serving aboard larger, cargo aircraft.

Eligibility also depends upon a servicemember meeting minimal time-in-flight requirements: four flight hours in a calendar month, or, eight flight hours in two consecutive calendar months, or, twelve fight hours in three consecutive months.

The same hour of flight cannot be counted more than once to meet minimum time-in-flight requirements for this version of flight pay.

When the unavailability of aircraft or military operations (including combat) makes it impossible for servicemembers to meet the minimum time-in-flight rules, commanders have the authority to widen the gate.

Rates: Eligible servicemembers receive Crewmember's Flight Pay at a monthly rate based upon rank.

The rates in effect for 1996 are as follows:

Rank	Rate
E-1	$110
E-2	110
E-3	110
E-4	125
E-5	150
E-6	175
E-7	200
E-8	200
E-9	200
W-1	125
W-2	150
W-3	175
W-4	250
W-5	250
O-1	125

O-2	150
O-3	175
O-4	225
O-5	250
O-6	250
O-7 & higher	110

Special Circumstances: A few special circumstances can have a dramatic effect upon servicemembers qualified for Crewmembers Flight Pay.

Hazardous Duties: Recipients of Crewmember Flight Pay can collect only one other pay that the military classifies as a Hazardous Duty Incentive Pay.

That category, discussed fully in chapter 7, "Hazardous Duty Pays," includes the following:
- Chemical Munitions Pay.
- Dangerous Organisms Pay.
- Demolition Duty Pay.
- Diving Pay.
- Experimental Stress Pay.
- Flight Deck Pay.
- Parachute Pay.
- Toxic Fuels Pay.
- Toxic Pesticides Pay.

Injury: When recipients of this bonus suffer flight-related injuries, they are eligible for this extra money for three months. In this category are people removed from flight status for "shock, derangement, or exhaustion" related to an aviation accident or their flight duties.

Eligibility for three months also continues if the injury resulted from hazardous duty to which the servicemember was ordered.

Incapacity from other causes doesn't similarly guarantee continued payments, although injured and ill servicemembers are entitled to the benefits of any "excess" flight hours.

NON-CREWMEMBERS FLIGHT PAY

People who aren't assigned to an aircraft or to flight duties may find themselves subject to, in the language of federal law, "frequent and regular participation in aerial flight, not as a crewmember."

Eligibility: Recipients are designated by their services. This isn't for servicemembers who fly a lot. It's listed by the military as a hazardous duty incentive pay.

Rates: Active-duty recipients receive $110 per month. Technically, performing a qualifying flight once a month should guarantee a full month's pay.

Reservists are eligible for one-thirtieth the rate—$3.67— for each day they qualify while on inactive-duty, or drill, status.

Restrictions: Recipients of other flight-related pays, such as ACIP, Crewmembers Flight Pay, and AWACS Pay are ineligible for Non-Crewmembers Flight Pay.

Recipients of Non-Crewmembers Flight Pay can receive only one other pay during a given month that the military classifies as a hazardous duty incentive pay. Also in this category are the following:

• Chemical Munitions Pay.
• Dangerous Organisms Pay.
• Demolition Duty Pay.
• Diving Pay.
• Experimental Stress Pay.
• Flight Deck Pay.
• Parachute Pay.
• Toxic Fuels Pay.
• Toxic Pesticides Pay.

AWACS FLIGHT PAY

Since the early 1980s, one of the most powerful weapons in the U.S. military arsenal doesn't have a single weapon aboard. It's the Airborne Warning and Control Systems (AWACS) aircraft, which are able to see the aerial battlefield and portions of the ground battlefield, and to bring the might of the U.S. air fleets into combat.

The people who serve aboard those AWACS aircraft are called air-weapons controller crewmembers. They have their own financial incentive to stay on active duty.

Eligibility: This special category of flight pay is available to commissioned officers, warrant officers, and enlisted people who are assigned to AWACS aircraft and take part in regular aerial operations.

Not eligible for this extra pay are enlisted members, warrant officers, other officers not assigned to AWACS duty, and crewmembers eligible for regular Flight Pay (ACIP), Crewmembers Flight Pay, or Non-Crewmembers Flight Pay.

Eligibility for AWACS Pay was opened up to warrant officers and enlisted members in January 1996.

Rates: AWACS Flight Pay is a monthly addition to the military paycheck. Amounts are determined by two factors—rank and the number of years of service as an air-weapons controller.

Maximum rates range from $125 monthly for people in the lowest enlisted ranks with more than 10 years on AWACS crews, to a maximum monthly rate of $350 for officers, $325 for warrant officers, and $300 for senior enlisted people.

TEN

NAVY PAYS

In This Chapter:
* *Sea Pay*
* *Submarine Pay*
* *Officers' Nuclear Pay*

* *Flight Deck Pay*
* *Commander's Responsibility Pay*

If you tried to find a single word that encapsulates the sacrifices of military life, from the physical dangers to the hardship of family separations and life with minimal privacy, probably the best single word is *Navy*.

Congress and the Pentagon have tried to provide financial recognition for the hazards and sacrifices of Navy life. Most of these payments are also open to Marines and Coast Guardsmen—and in fact, to soldiers and airmen—if they meet the requirements.

SEA PAY
Most military members serving aboard naval vessels can receive a substantial addition to their monthly paychecks to make up

for some of hazards and hardships of shipboard service in form of monthly Sea Pay.

Sea Pay Summary:	
Purpose:	Financial recognition for hardships, hazards
Amounts:	$50 to $520 monthly (1996)
Formula:	By rank, time at sea
Taxable:	Yes
Loopholes:	Add-on Sea Pay Premium
Problem Areas:	Rates based on continuous service at sea.

Actually, there are two kinds of Sea Pay. Both will be discussed in this section. What we'll call simple Sea Pay is technically known as Career Sea Pay. There's another kind of Sea Pay for folks who've spent some time with the fleet. We'll refer to it as Sea Pay Premium; its formal name is Career Sea Pay Premium.

Eligibility: Sea Pay is given to E-4s, enlisted members in higher ranks, officers, and warrant officers of the active-duty force and the reserve components.

Reservists must be drawing Basic Pay during any period for which they also draw Sea Pay. Commissioned officers are ineligible for Sea Pay for their first 36 months of sea-duty. E-1s, E-2s, and E-3s are ineligible.

Concerning assignment, Sea Pay recipients must fall into one of these categories:

• Permanently assigned to a ship, a ship-based staff, or a ship-based aviation unit. The ship's primary mission must be accomplished at sea.

• Temporarily assigned to a ship, a ship-based staff, or a ship-based aviation unit. The ship's primary mission must be accomplished at sea.

- Crews of submarines that have two crews, both the "on-crew" serving at sea and the "off-crew."
- Crews of submarine tenders and destroyer tenders.

Rates: Amounts of monthly Sea Pay are set by charts that reflect a servicemember's rank and the number of years that person has accumulated of "sea duty."

For enlisted folks, the rates start at $50 per month for an E-4 with less than 1 year's sea duty, and they peak at $520 monthly for an E-9 with over 16 years of sea duty.

For warrant officers, the rates range from $130 monthly for a W-1 with less than a year's sea duty to $500 monthly for W-4s with more than 18 years' sea duty.

For commissioned officers, the rates begin at $150 monthly for O-1s, O-2s, and O-3s with more than 3 years' sea duty. The top rate for commissioned officers is $380 monthly for O-6s.

Slightly higher rates go to people who were on active duty or drawing Sea Pay between October 1, 1987, and May 1, 1988.

Sea Pay Premium: In addition to regular Sea Pay, some servicemembers are eligible for an extra monthly payment of $100 called Sea Pay Premium.

It's for consecutive months of sea duty. Note the word *consecutive.* That means one month after another.

Sea Pay Premium is keyed to sea duty, not Sea Pay, an important distinction for commissioned officers, who don't receive Sea Pay for their first three years of sea duty.

E-4s, commissioned officers, and warrant officers begin receiving the Sea Pay Premium on their 37th consecutive month of sea duty.

E-5s, E-6s, E-7s, E-8s, and E-9s lose Sea Pay Premium after sixty-one consecutive months of sea duty.

Special Circumstances: Here's how the rules about Sea Pay and Sea Pay Premium affect servicemembers facing special situations.

Confinement: Servicemembers suspended from their duties or confined awaiting court-martial or civilian trials lose their Sea Pay and Sea Pay Premium at the start of their confinement or suspension. Those extra pays are restored retroactively if the servicemember is acquitted or the charges are dismissed.

Leave: Recipients of Sea Pay continue to receive it while on leave.

Nonjudicial Punishment: Sea Pay recipients who are punished at a Captain's Mast continue receiving extra money for their sea duty.

Temporary Duty: Sea Pay recipients retain eligibility for the extra money for the first 30 days of temporary additional duty ashore.

SUBMARINE PAY

With the exception of astronauts in outer space, the group of humans beings who live and work in the next-least-habitable environment are the people assigned to submarines.

Submarine Pay Summary:	
Purpose:	Financial recognition for hardships and skills
Amounts:	Enlisted: $75 monthly to $355 (1996)
	Warrant: $310 to $355 monthly
	Officer: $175 to $595 monthly
Formula:	By rank, time in submarine fleet
Taxable:	Yes
Loopholes:	Also eligible for Sea Pay

Submarine Pay is technically known as Incentive Pay for Operational Submarine Duty. There is a second kind of pay for long-time members of the "silent service." It's discussed in this section and identified as Submarine Continuation Pay, although its technical name is Continuous Monthly Submarine Duty Incentive Pay.

Eligibility: Submarine Pay is available to enlisted personnel, warrant officers, and commissioned officers, both on active duty and in the reserves.

Generally, recipients of Submarine Pay must be assigned to a submarine. This includes the following:

• Crew members of operating submarines.

• Folks training to serve on nuclear-powered submarines.

• Personnel training for more advanced submarine duties.

• People training for increased responsibilities on a submarine.

Eligibility also extends to qualified submariners on shore-based staffs of submarine headquarters who meet certain criteria, roughly involving 48 underway hours per month.

Submariners who aren't directly assigned to submarines—and therefore ineligible for Sea Pay—may qualify for Submarine *Continuation* Pay, discussed separately below.

Rates: Submarine Pay is a monthly addition to the military paycheck. Amounts are based on rank and time in service, not time in submarines.

Rates are shown in charts identical in format to the Basic Pay charts. Here are the two ends of that time-in-service spectrum for each rank:

	Under 2 Years	Over 26 Years
E-1	$ 75	$ 75
E-2	75	90
E-3	80	90
E-4	80	175
E-5	140	195

E-6	155	265
E-7	225	310
E-8	225	345
E-9	225	355
W-1	235	355
W-2	235	355
W-3	235	355
W-4	235	355
W-5	235	355
O-1	175	355
O-2	235	355
O-3	355	595
O-4	365	595
O-5	595	595
O-6	595	595
O-7	355	355
O-8	355	355
O-9	355	355
O-10	355	355

Keep in mind that these are the highest and lowest rates of Submarine Pay for each rank.

Submarine Continuation Pay: Servicemembers who are qualified as submariners can receive Submarine Continuation Pay when they're not assigned to a submarine or to the staff of a submarine command.

The rates for Submarine Continuation Pay are the same ones used for Submarine Pay.

Generally, Submarine Continuation Pay stops at the end of a submariner's 26th year in the military or whenever that person is receiving regular Submarine Pay. To qualify, military members must spend at least six years assigned to submarines during the first 12 years as a qualified submariner or at least 10 years assigned to submarines during the first 18 years as a qualified submariner.

Folks who don't meet the 6-in-12 rule and who fall short of the 10-in-18 rule can qualify for Submarine Continuation Pay until the end of their 22nd year in the military if they spend at least eight years assigned to submarines during their first 18 years as a qualified submariner.

Special Circumstances: Here's how the rules about Submarine Pay and Submarine Continuation Pay affect servicemembers facing special situations.

Enlisted Only: Enlisted members in nonsubmarine shore billets lose their right to Submarine Continuation Pay if they have insufficient time left in their enlistments for another tour of submarine duty.

Leave: While on leave, Submarine Pay and Submarine Continuation Pay continue.

Officers Only: For officers who were previously enlisted, their enlisted time is subtracted from their total time in service for computation of Submarine Pay and Submarine Continuation Pay.

An officer who turns down an appointment as an executive officer or commanding officer of a submarine loses all rights to Submarine Pay and Submarine Continuation Pay except when serving on a submarine under way. That also applies to an officer who's officially listed as "failed selection" for assignment to one of those key posts.

Reserves: Reservists who are performing weekend drills, or more technically, on inactive-duty status, are eligible to receive Submarine Pay. They are entitled to one-thirtieth of the monthly rate. Reservists on inactive-duty status are ineligible for Submarine Continuation Pay.

Temporary Duty: While on temporary additional duty, Submarine Pay continues for people assigned to submarines. Submarine Continuation Pay also continues for people on temporary additional duty.

However, people assigned to shore-based staffs who must spend a certain amount of time under way to maintain eligibility for Submarine Pay must still meet those time-underway rules to continue receiving the extra money in their paychecks.

OFFICERS' NUCLEAR PAY

As a general rule, officers don't get bonuses for coming on active duty or agreeing to stay in uniform a little longer. Like all general rules, this one has exceptions. One of the more unusual exceptions involves officers qualified to oversee nuclear-propulsion systems.

Officers' Nuclear Pay Summary:	
Purpose:	Recruit and retain nuclear-propulsion experts
Amounts:	Lump-sum $2,000 to $10,000 annually (1996)
Formula:	Several different programs
Taxable:	Yes
Problem Areas:	Repay if don't meet commitment.

These so-called nuclear-qualified officers are eligible for four different sign-up programs. Two are financial incentives to draw officers into the field; two are incentives to keep those officers in the specialty and on active duty.

Basics: Whatever the specific incentive program, the Navy's bonuses for nuclear specialists within its commissioned ranks share several features:

• All bonuses are for officers in—or training for—duties involving "the supervision, operation, and maintenance of naval nuclear propulsion plants."

• Recipients must be specifically selected by the Navy, undergo technical training, and agree to serve fixed amounts of time on active duty.

• Recipients who fail to serve their obligated time may have to repay the military for the payment.

Junior Officer Sign-Up Bonus: Called the Nuclear Officer Accession Bonus, it targets officers with less than five years' commissioned service. It's also open to would-be officers. Recipients are eligible for a one-time bonus of $4,000.

Mid-Career Sign-Up Bonus: A larger-scoped program, called the Nuclear Career Accession Bonus is available to officers who are officially classified as "unrestricted-line officers."

At the end of training as nuclear-qualified officers, they're entitled to a one-time payment of $2,000.

Nuclear Continuation Pay: Officers in the nuclear field can apply for Nuclear-Qualified Officer Extending Period of Active Service Pay, or, as it's better known, Nuclear Continuation Pay. Applicants must be qualified in the field.

If accepted, officers can receive up to $10,000 per year, for formal commitments to stay three, four, or five years on active duty within the nuclear field.

Applications must be made before the officer's 23rd anniversary of commissioned service. Payments cannot continue beyond the officer's 26th anniversary of commissioning.

Annual Incentive Bonus: Some nuclear-qualified officers who don't receive Nuclear Continuation Pay are eligible for another annual bonus. Basically, it's a year-by-year financial incentive to officers unwilling to commit to a multiyear contract.

Called Nuclear Career Annual Incentive Bonus, it provides

annual lump-sum payments of $7,200 to officers technically classified as "unrestricted line" and $3,600 for commissioned officers and warrant officers who are listed as "limited-duty officers."

FLIGHT DECK PAY

One of the most dangerous places on the planet is the flight deck of an aircraft carrier when planes are taking off or landing.

Flight Deck Pay Summary:	
Purpose:	Financial recognition for extra risks
Amounts:	$110 monthly (1996)
Formula:	One rate for everyone
Taxable:	Yes
Loopholes:	Qualifying for four days gives month's pay
Problem Areas:	Formal assignment to unit, billet

The military has long had a special pay category for the men and women whose jobs put them in that dangerous spot. Technically, Flight Deck Pay is classified by the military as a hazardous duty incentive pay, covered by the same general rules as items listed in chapter 7, "Hazardous Duty Pays."

Eligibility: Flight-Deck Pay is available to officers, warrant officers and enlisted members from the active-duty force, plus members of the reserves who meet other eligibility requirements.

Recipients must be assigned to the crew of an aircraft carrier capable of fixed-wing landings and takeoffs, or to an aviation unit with fixed-wing aircraft that operates from aircraft carriers. (Members of helicopter units and vessels carrying helicopters don't qualify for Flight Deck Pay.)

Further, the servicemember's official military duties must require their presence on the flight deck during takeoffs and landings. Further still, military folks must participate at least four days in a calendar month in actual takeoffs and landings. Military members on temporary duty with aviation units or aircraft carriers can qualify for Flight Deck Pay if ordered to serve in a job normally designated for the extra money.

Rates: The monthly rate of Flight Deck Pay for all recipients is $110.

Double-Pay Restrictions: Recipients of Flight Deck Pay can receive, simultaneously, Hostile Fire Pay or Imminent Danger Pay. But they cannot receive for the same calendar month any another kind of extra pay that the military officially categorizes as Hostile Fire Incentive Pay. Those pays are listed in chapter 7, "Hazardous Duty Pays."

COMMANDER'S RESPONSIBILITY PAY

In 1958, Congress authorized a special monthly addition to the paycheck, known unofficially as Responsibility Pay, as a financial incentive to keep enough officers in the (then) high-tech fields. Responsibility Pay is still around—at the original 1958 rates.

Responsibility Pay Summary:

Purpose:	Extra money for officers in command slots
Amounts:	$50 to $150 monthly (1996)
Formula:	By rank
Taxable:	Yes
Problem Areas:	Not for medical officers; token payment

Responsibility Pay is used only by the Navy and Coast Guard, and only then for officers in command assignments. Its formal name is Special Pay for Officers Serving in Positions of Unusual Responsibility and of a Critical Nature.

Eligibility: Recipients of Responsibility Pay must be officers permanently and formally assigned to positions of command.

The Navy maintains a list of billets that qualify. Generally, if an officer is entitled to wear the Command-at-Sea pin, that person is eligible for Responsibility Pay.

For Coast Guard officers, most vessel commanders qualify.

Officers temporarily in command of units are ineligible, even when the permanent occupier of a command slot is entitled to the extra money.

Responsibility Pay may not be paid to anyone in the rank of O-7 or in a higher rank. Nor may the money be paid to medical officers, regardless of their position.

Rates: Monthly amounts are based strictly upon rank, as follows:

O-3	$ 50
O-4	50
O-5	100
O-6	150

Payments continue as long as an officer is permanently assigned to a qualifying command slot. Neither eligibility nor rates are affected when recipients take leave or go on temporary duty away from their commands.

ELEVEN

RESERVE PAYS

In This Chapter:
- *Extended Active-Duty Pay*
- *Other Activity-Duty Pay*
- *Inactive-Duty Pay*
- *Sign-up Bonuses*
- *Other Pays*
- *Uniform Allowances*
- *Incapacitation Pay*

Some of the most important members of the military don't wear a uniform every day. Reservists and National Guardsmen assume important tasks for the military. Fortunately, a network of financial programs are already available to meet their needs.

In this chapter, the term *reservist* includes members of the National Guard. In the few instances when the rules apply differently to members of the reserves and members of the National Guard, that distinction is clearly made.

EXTENDED ACTIVE-DUTY PAY
When a member of the reserves or National Guard is officially

classified as being "on extended active duty," that person is treated by the pay office the same as any other active-duty member.

Usually, a reservist's eligibility for Basic Pay, Basic Allowance for Quarters (BAQ), and Basic Allowance for Subsistence (BAS) begins when he or she leaves home to report to the first duty station.

Members of the National Guard called to federal service begin their eligibility for military pay when they appear at the place officially designated for the company rendezvous, or the equivalent.

The rules for the start date of other elements of a military paycheck vary with each benefit.

OTHER ACTIVE-DUTY PAY

Between the clear-cut extremes of reservists on extended active duty and those on inactive duty, as weekend drill periods are called, is a wide-ranging group of reservists and Guardsmen. They are officially classified as the following:

- Active duty training.
- Active duty for training.
- Full-time training duty.
- Annual training duty.
- Attendance at service school.

Generally, these servicemembers are entitled by law to receive military pay and allowances in accordance with their rank, years of service, and dependency status.

Some very specific provisions affect them in ways different from active-duty and inactive-duty folks.

Active Duty without Pay: Military members may be brought on active duty without pay. This can only be done with the servicemember's consent. "Without pay" means without Basic Pay.

Some folks are asked by the military to serve on active duty "without allowances." This means without the Basic Allowance for Quarters and the Basic Allowance for Subsistence. Reservists and Guardsmen may find it's in their interest to come on active duty without pay for short periods to attend important classes or earn points for retirement.

Allotments: Servicemembers voluntarily serving on active duty for less than 180 days, or involuntarily on active duty for less than 24 months, are usually ineligible to direct their military finance center to send portions of their military pay—formally known as allotments—to another person or agency.

Exceptions are National Guardsmen. They can make allotments to pay premiums for group life insurance that's sponsored by their state organizations.

Double Pay: Anyone receiving active-duty pay is ineligible for Drill Pay, or Inactive-Duty Pay, for that day.

Military retirees must waive a day of retired pay, or keep their retired pay while waiving a day of active-duty pay, for each day on active duty. Recipients of VA disability compensation must waive a day of their VA money, or keep the VA money while waiving a day of active-duty pay, for each day on active duty.

Leave: Anyone who serves on active duty for at least 30 consecutive days is entitled to 2.5 days of military leave for each month.

If the leave hasn't been used by the time the reservist leaves active duty, it can be cashed in. Military members receive one-thirtieth of Basic Pay for each cashed-in leave day. No other kinds of military pay—such as BAQ, BAS, or special pays—are counted.

Other Pays: In addition to Basic Pay, BAQ, and BAS, reservists and National Guardsmen are eligible for other kinds of military pay, assuming they meet the necessary eligibility rules, including the following:

- Crewmembers Flight Pay.
- Family Separation Allowance.
- Flight Pay (ACIP).
- Foreign Duty Pay.
- Non-Crewmembers Flight Pay.
- Overseas Cost-of-Living Allowance.
- Overseas Housing Allowance.
- Parachute Pay.
- Sea Pay.
- Special Duty Assignment Pay.
- Temporary Lodging Allowance.
- Variable Housing Allowance.

Rates: Reservists and National Guardsmen on active duty (under this nonextended duty category) are entitled to Basic Pay, the Basic Allowance for Quarters, and the Basic Allowance for Subsistence at the rates appropriate for their rank, years of service, and dependents, using the same rates as the regular active-duty force.

However, for the first and last months on active duty, these people are paid the monthly benefits at a daily rate—that is, one-thirtieth of the monthly rate for each day on active duty.

INACTIVE-DUTY PAY

Reservists and National Guardsmen on inactive-duty training—as the familiarly known weekend drill periods are formally called—have their own pay chart.

Inactive-Duty Pay, or drill pay, goes to reservists and National Guardsmen who fall within one of several major categories, including these:

- Inactive-duty training.
- Unit training assembly (UTA).
- Additional flying training period (AFTP).
- Additional inactive-duty training.
- Other equivalent training, instruction, or duty.

Inactive Duty Pay Summary:

Purpose:	Pay for time and tasks during drill periods
Amounts:	$26.90 to $300.50 per drill period (1996)
Rates:	By rank, years of service
Taxable:	Yes
Loopholes:	Pay can exceed 360 days per year
Problem Areas:	Same-day active-duty pay

To get paid, reservists must spend a fixed amount of time—usually four hours—performing duties or training approved in advance by their parent service.

Active Duty: A military member cannot receive Basic Pay and Inactive-Duty Pay for the same calendar day.

Reservists and guardsmen who spend part of a calendar year on active duty and part drawing Inactive-Duty Pay can receive the equivalent of more than 360 days' Basic Pay during a single calendar year. (Keep in mind that one day's Basic Pay is paid for each drill period, and typically reservists and Guardsmen train for two drill periods each day.)

Active Duty without Pay: Military members may be brought on inactive duty without pay. This can be done only with the servicemember's consent, usually to earn retirement points or attend key training.

Allotments: Usually, reservists and National Guardsmen are ineligible to direct their military finance center to send portions of their Inactive-Duty Pay—formally known as allotments—to another person or agency.

An exception are National Guardsmen. They can make allotments from Inactive-Duty Pay to pay premiums for group life insurance that's sponsored by their state organizations.

Leave: People drawing Inactive-Duty Pay don't accumulate any credit toward military leave for that time on the government payroll.

Other Pays: In addition to Inactive-Duty Pay, reservists and National Guardsmen on drill status are eligible for other kinds of military pay, assuming they meet the necessary eligibility rules, including the following:

- Demolition Pay.
- Diving Pay.
- Experimental Stress Pay.
- Flight Deck Pay.
- Flight Pay (ACIP).
- Foreign Language Pay.
- Parachute Pay.
- Submarine Pay.

Rates: When it comes to Inactive-Duty Pay, the military measures time by the drill period. Basic Pay for each drill period is equal to one-thirtieth of the monthly Basic Pay for the appropriate rank and year of service for each person.

Officially, a drill period is at least two hours long. Frequently, it's four hours.

Regardless of the actual amount of time spent on inactive-duty jobs or training, reservists and Guardsmen can be paid only for two drill periods during a calendar day.

Retirees: Military retirees must waive a day of their retired pay for each day of Inactive-Duty Pay. The waiver is based upon days, not formal drill periods. Military retirees don't have the options to keep the retired pay and waive the drill pay.

Recipients of VA disability compensation must waive two days' of VA money for each day of Inactive-Duty Pay. That's based on the notion that two drill periods occur in one normal training day.

SIGN-UP BONUSES

Most people join the military for a mixture of reasons. Patriotism is a part of the mixture, and so is financial self-interest.

The armed forces have always offered financial incentives

for people to join—or stay in—the reserves and National Guard. A variety of programs are available to help nudge them closer to a decision to stay a little longer in uniform.

Enlistment: A sign-up bonus is offered to people who agree to become enlisted members in a drilling reserve unit or in the trained manpower pool known as the Individual Mobilization Augmentees.

Called Enlistment Bonus for the Selective Reserve, this program offers bonuses up to $5,000. The actual amount varies by service and by specialty. Candidates must be high school graduates who never served in the military and be willing to serve at least six years.

"Critical Specialties" Forgiveness: Enlisted members who enter the reserves or National Guard with certain federally backed student loans may be eligible to have the military pay off those debts if they meet certain criteria:

• Reservists must possess a skill that the parent service recognizes as a "critical specialty."

• Reservists must agree to serve with a drilling reserve unit or as a member of the manpower pool known as the Individual Mobilization Augmentee program.

• The loan must be one of a handful of federally funded or federally insured student loans. Eligible loans are specifically identified in the federal law establishing this repayment bonus.

For each year of service, the government will repay either 15 percent of the outstanding loan or $500, whichever is more.

Prior-Service Enlistment: People who have already served on active duty may qualify for a Prior-Service Enlistment Bonus if they have the right military skills and agree to join a drilling reserve unit or the trained manpower pool known as the Individual Mobilization Augmentees.

This bonus is $2,500 for a three-year commitment and $5,000 for a six-year commitment. Participants must:

- Have less than 10 years total military time.
- Possess an honorable discharge.
- Possess a military skill for which the bonus is offered.
- Not have previously received any reserve-related enlistment bonus, reenlistment payment, or extension of service pay.

Recipients who don't serve the agreed-upon period must repay the government for time not spent.

IRR/ING Enlistment: The Individual Ready Reserve (IRR) and the Inactive National Guard (ING) are collections of trained, experienced personnel who aren't assigned either to a unit or to a job they'll fill if mobilized.

Up to $1,500 can be paid to people who go straight into the IRR or ING. Participants must:

- Not have served before in the military.
- Enlist for six years.
- Qualify in a combat or combat support skill.

Prior-Service "Affiliation" Bonus: Enlisted people with previous active-duty experience who agree to join a drilling reserve unit or who possess skills specifically sought by one of the services can receive a $50 monthly Affiliation Bonus.

Participants must:

- Be eligible for reenlistment in the active-duty force.
- Agree to serve with a reserve unit or possess a needed skill.
- Have a rank and skill for which the parent service has vacancies.
- Agree to serve with a reserve unit or in the trained manpower pool known as the Individual Mobilization Augmentees for the rest of their obligated time.

Note that the Affiliation Bonus, in itself, doesn't add time to one's military obligations.

This bonus isn't available to people joining the reserves or the National Guard to be full-time technicians.

Reenlistment Bonus: Extra money, called the Selected Reserve Reenlistment Bonus, is available to qualified people who agree to spend more time in a drilling reserve unit or the trained manpower pool known as Individual Mobilization Augmentees.

This bonus is $1,250 for a three-year commitment and $2,500 for a six-year commitment. Participants must:

• Have less than 10 years total military time.

• Possess a military skill—or agree to join a certain unit—for which the bonus is offered.

• Not have previously received any reserve-related enlistment bonus, reenlistment payment, or extension of service pay.

Enlisted members can receive this bonus only once during their military careers.

IRR/ING Reenlistment Bonus: Experienced reservists and guardsmen who aren't assigned either to a unit for regular drills or to a specific job that they'd be expected to fill if mobilized can qualify for a sign-up bonus by joining—or staying in—one of two important manpower pools.

The Individual Ready Reserve (IRR) and the Inactive National Guard (ING) can offer a one-time bonus up to $1,500 for people who reenlist or voluntarily extend their commitments to stay in the IRR or the ING. Participants must:

• Sign up for either three years or six years.

• Not have any remaining time-in-service obligations.

• Qualify in a combat or combat-support skill.

Six-year commitments may bring a bonus of $1,500. A three-year commitment brings a maximum of $750.

Health Professionals' Loan Forgiveness: In order to persuade health professionals to join the reserves and National Guard, the services have the authority to repay some of their educational loans.

Participants must be officers serving with drilling reserve units or as members of the manpower pool known as the Individual Mobilization Augmentee program. Also, they must possess skills that the military considers critical in wartime.

There are few restrictions on the kind of loan that will be repaid, so long as it was used to finance professional education in the critical skill.

The maximum annual repayment is $3,000, with a $20,000 lifetime limit per person.

"DEP" Protection: People who enlist in the reserves through the Delayed Entry Program can have lengthy waits between the time they agree to join the military and the time they actually come on active duty for training.

They're guaranteed the size of the enlistment bonus that was offered at the time they joined the DEP.

OTHER PAYS

At least two bonuses available to members of the reserve components don't have a counterpart among the active-duty force.

Muster Pay: The services may call reservists and National Guardsmen to a reserve center for a one-day examination of records and a quick physical examination. Muster Pay is what those folks get for their efforts.

Ineligible for Muster Pay are National Guardsmen, members of drilling reserve units, and members of the Individual Mobilization Augmentation Program.

Recipients must be present at least two hours at their assigned locations. They are ineligible for any active-duty pay or inactive-duty pay for a day when they receive Muster Pay. It can be paid only once a year to an individual.

Everyone receives the same amount of Muster Pay. The amount, which varies slightly from year to year, was $99.15 in 1995.

From that is subtracted federal and state income tax and 50 cents for Servicemen's Group Life Insurance. No Social Security taxes are withheld from Muster Pay. Muster Pay must be paid on the day of the muster or before.

"High Priority" Unit Pay: In order to attract and maintain people in units with a high likelihood of being mobilized during emergencies, the services can offer a financial incentive.

Called High Priority or Designated Unit Pay, it's available only to enlisted personnel. Recipients must be in a reserve unit that's been designated by the parent service for the extra pay. Payments are authorized for:

- Regular inactive-duty—or drill—periods.
- Unit training assemblies.
- Equivalent training or instruction lasting at least four hours.

Enlisted members of a designated unit may draw the pay for duties performed with another unit, whose members aren't entitled to High Priority Unit Pay. But folks from ineligible units can't receive the extra money when they serve with one of the designated units.

The amount is set at $10 per drill period for everyone. Since the normal weekend drill consists of two official drill periods per day for two days, qualified reservists will see an extra $40 in their paychecks for a weekend's service.

The money is subject to federal and state income taxes. No Social Security tax is withheld from that payment.

UNIFORM ALLOWANCES

Typically, reservists and National Guardsmen receive uniform allowances appropriate for their service—or the actual uniform items themselves—when first coming on active duty for their initial training.

The general rule is that they don't receive any other uniform allowances throughout their careers in the reserve components. That's the general rule. But there are exceptions.

Navy Allowances: Enlisted members of the naval reserve may find themselves eligible for special uniform allowances at two points in their careers.

New E-7s: Enlisted members newly promoted to E-7 are eligible for a one-time uniform allowance to purchase special uniform items. This also applies to E-7s who never received this allowance when assigned to drilling units.

The 1996 rate is $360. The actual amount varies from year to year.

E7s and Higher: A quarterly uniform allowance is payable to some members of the naval reserve in the ranks of E-7, E-8, and E-9.

Officially called the Reserve Quarterly Maintenance Clothing Allowance, it goes to senior enlisted members who participate in at least 75 percent of their units' scheduled drill periods.

The quarterly amount is $9. It's paid only to enlisted members who qualify for a full quarter. Fractional payments aren't authorized.

Officers: Reserve and National Guard officers can qualify for a uniform allowance under two major circumstances. Some people qualify for both at the same time.

Initial: Reserve component officers receive a one-time $200 uniform allowance after 14 days on active duty for training or after 14 drill periods while on inactive duty.

If reserve or National Guard officers had previously received the $200, the only time they can receive a second payment is if they switch to another branch of the military.

Active-Duty: Reserve component officers returning to active duty for at least 90 days can qualify for a $100 uniform allowance to bring their wardrobe up to snuff.

Ineligible are officers who have received their initial $200 uniform allowances within the previous two years. Also ineligible are those returning to active duty after periods away that are less than two years.

Women-Only Allowances: Enlisted female members of the reserve components may be entitled to a one-time initial cash allowance if they were unable to receive appropriate underclothing and other personal items through official supply channels when they first came on active duty.

INCAPACITATION PAY

If a military member's health is harmed by service in the armed forces, then the U.S. government is supposed to provide medical care and financial help. That's been a basic principle in the United States for a long time.

Incapacitation Pay Summary:	
Purpose:	Offset financial losses of injury, illness
Amounts:	Varies on case-by-case basis
Formula:	Percentage of Basic Pay, BAQ, BAS
Taxable:	Yes
Problem Areas:	AWOL; court-martial; divorce

Reservists and Guardsmen on active duty are covered by the same financial safety nets as members of the active-duty force. For reservists and National Guardsmen who don't qualify for active-duty protections, there is Incapacitation Pay.

Eligibility: Recipients must be members of the reserves or National Guard on active duty for 30 days or less, on inactive duty, or traveling directly to or from inactive duty or active duty of 30 days or less.

The medical problem for which Incapacitation Pay is sought must be an injury, illness, or disease that was caused or aggravated when the reservist was in one of the three eligibility periods mentioned above.

Specifically not eligible, under federal law, are reservists hurt during correspondence courses or while officially classified as being "on inactive status" to attend an educational program sponsored by one of the armed forces.

Rates: The amount of Incapacitation Pay is calculated according to a two-step process.

First, it begins with the Basic Pay, BAQ, and BAS that the servicemember would receive on active duty.

Second, from that figure is subtracted any other job-related income, including sick leave, vacation pay, and payments from income-protection plans.

If recipients of Incapacitation Pay are able to earn some civilian income, Incapacitation Pay is reduced to fill in the gap between what they made in their civilian jobs before their injury and what they're able earn afterwards.

Under no circumstances can Incapacitation Pay exceed the amount of Basic Pay, BAQ, and BAS that a reservist or National Guardsman would receive on active duty.

It ends after six months. People still in need of financial assistance for their injuries after six months can seek VA Disability Compensation. (See Chapter 18, "Retirement and Disability Pays".)

TWELVE

MEDICAL PAYS

In This Chapter:
- *Key Definition*
- *Special Pay for Doctors*
- *Special Pay for Dentists*
- *Special Pay for Nurses*

- *Special Pay for Veterinarians and Optometrists*

For the health professionals who care for military members, their families, and retirees, the government has put together an intricate package of special bonuses. Some are token financial recognition for their sacrifices. Others are hard-nosed incentives designed to ensure that the armed forces have the right mix of medical professionals.

What follows is a summary of the major financial programs affecting health care professionals. This is not an exhaustive collection of details.

KEY DEFINITION

The same phrase pops up in the eligibility rules for many medically related bonuses. It's *creditable service*. For most, this is time spent on active duty in the medical corps of the Army, the Medical Corps of the Navy, or as an Air Force medical officer.

Creditable service also includes time spent on internships and residencies, even if they occurred when a physician had no connection whatsoever with the military. The only catch for having internships or residencies counted as creditable service is that they must have been successfully completed.

Time spent on internships and residencies that were not successfully completed can also count as creditable time if they ended because of a military operation.

Time in foreign institutions not accredited by the standard accrediting bodies does not count.

SPECIAL PAY FOR DOCTORS

A group with the largest financial gap between them and their civilian counterparts are the men and women of the armed forces who hold medical degrees. Six different kinds of extra pay, each designed to solve a particular manpower shortage or right a glaring monetary inequity, are on the books.

Variable Special Pay: Most medical officers of the Army, Navy, and Air Force are eligible for this category of special pay that narrows the financial gap for many professionals, with a special eye on midcareer officers.

Eligibility: Usually, a doctor must be committed to at least one year on active duty to receive Variable Special Pay. That limit was waived for the Persian Gulf War.

Eligibility isn't affected by any other kind of military pay or medically related additions to the military paycheck.

Rates: Here are the rates in effect for Variable Special Pay in 1996. All time is measured in creditable years, as discussed above:

- Serving as an intern—$100.
- Less than six years—$416.
- At least six years, but less than eight—$1,000.
- At least eight years, but less than 10—$958.
- At least 10 years, but less than 12—$916.

- At least 12 years, but less than 14—$833.
- At least 14 years, but less than 18—$750.
- At least 18 years, but less than 22—$666.
- 22 years or more—$583.

Medical officers who are generals in the Army, Air Force, or Marine Corps or admirals in the Navy receive $583 monthly, regardless of creditable service.

Board Certified Pay: Increasingly, the medical community and ordinary patients expect physicians to be board certified. That means they've passed special examinations given for their medical specialty and they maintain the professional standards set by the governing board for each major specialty.

Board-Certified Pay is the military's special incentive to encourage physicians in uniform to become—and to stay— board certified.

Eligibility: There are two eligibility hoops through which physicians must pass. First, they must qualify for Variable Special Pay, discussed above. Second, they must be board certified.

The board certifications must come from a body recognized by the American Board of Medical Specialties or the Advisory Board for Osteopathic Specialists. An exception involves physicians in specialties unique to military medicine for which no formal postgraduate training program exists.

Key Definition: See the discussion of creditable service in the "Key Definition" section of this chapter.

Rates: Here are the monthly rates for Board-Certified Pay that were in effect for 1996. All references to years refer to creditable service:

- Less than 10 years—$208.
- At least 10 years, but less than 12—$291.
- At least 12 years, but less than 14—$333.
- At least 14 years, but less than 18—$416.
- 18 years or more—$500.

The rates for Board-Certified Pay don't change every year. In fact, there's no fixed pattern for their improvement.

Additional Special Pay: To persuade military doctors nearing the end of their obligated time in uniform to stay around a little longer, Additional Special Pay provides an extra financial incentive.

Eligibility: Additional Special Pay is available to medical doctors of the Army, Navy, and Air Force who sign a formal agreement to stay in the military at least one year more than their current obligations. The time limit can be waived for physicians supporting Persian Gulf operations. Not eligible are interns and people undergoing initial residency training.

Rates: Additional Special Pay comes in one size—$15,000. Doctors qualify for $15,000 for each 12-month period for which they agree to serve. Payments are made in lump sums beginning at the start of each 12-month period.

Repayment: Additional Special Pay is an advance payment, and many factors may keep a doctor from serving the length of the obligation. Physicians who leave the military before completing their obligations may have to repay the government for unearned payments.

Incentive Special Pay: Many military assignments don't provide physicians with the opportunities for professional growth that doctors commonly experience in the civilian world. Incentive Special Pay is one of the military's tools for balancing that scale.

Eligibility: Eligibility is decided by two sets of factors. One involves the doctor, the other the needs of the service.

Recipients must sign a formal agreement to stay in the military at least one year more than their current obligation.

As far as the service is concerned, the military authorizes Incentive Special Pay for physicians in critical specialties, or doctors who are the only professional in their specialty at a particular assignment, or physicians at assignments with no opportunities for continuing professional education or positions isolated from the medical community.

Rates: Incentive Special Pay has a maximum payment of $36,000 for each year of service. The military frequently offers physicians a lesser amount. Whatever the size, payments are made in a lump sum at the start of each 12-month period.

Repayment: Incentive Special Pay is an advance payment, and many factors may keep a doctor from serving the length of the obligation. Physicians who leave the military before completing their obligations may have to repay the government for unearned payments.

Special Pay for Reservists: Medical doctors who are reservists serving with reserve units are ineligible for many of the special pays discussed earlier in this chapter, but there is one pay program tailored for reserve physicians.

Eligibility: Medical doctors of the Army, Navy, or Air Force serving on active duty for periods less than one year are eligible for a program with the lengthy official name of Special Pay for Active Duty of Reserve Medical Officers. They're only eligible while on active duty.

Rates: This special program for reserve physicians offers $450 per month over and above their regular pays and allowances.

Key Detail: Any reserve physician committed to spending at least a year on active duty may be eligible for any of the other incentive payments for doctors that are discussed in this chapter.

Multiyear Special Pay: As the name of this special program announces, its goal is to provide a financial incentive for physicians to agree formally to longer stretches on active duty.

Eligibility: To qualify for this addition to a military paycheck, active-duty physicians cannot be a brigadier general, rear admiral (lower half), or a higher rank.

Participants must have completed at least eight years of creditable service, which was defined in detail earlier in this chapter.

Rates: Amounts are set by specialty and by the number of years of additional service. For 1996, the rates ranged from $2,000 per year to $14,000 per year. Not all specialties qualified.

Counting Time: Recipients of Multiyear Special Pay may receive other medically related bonuses that require them to serve a certain amount of time on active duty. That time can be "paid back" simultaneously with the time served to fulfill an obligation for Multiyear Special Pay.

Repayment: Multiyear Special Pay is an advance payment, and many factors may keep a doctor from serving the length of the obligation. Physicians who leave the military before completing their obligations may have to repay the government for unearned payments.

SPECIAL PAY FOR DENTISTS

Like physicians, dentists on active duty experience a large financial gap between their incomes and the salaries of their civilian counterparts. To minimize that financial discrepancy, three different kinds of special pay for dentists have been created, each designed to solve a particular manpower problem.

Variable Special Pay: Most dental officers of the Army, Navy, and Air Force are eligible for Variable Special Pay, which offsets the financial loss for officers who aren't necessarily committed to spending 20 years in uniform.

Eligibility: Usually, a military dentist must be committed to at least one year on active duty to receive Variable Special Pay. That limit was waived for the Persian Gulf War.

Rates: Here are the monthly rates in effect for Variable Special Pay in 1996. Again, all time is measured in creditable service years, as discussed above:

- Serving as an intern or with less than three years—$100.
- At least three but less than six years—$166.
- At least six years, but less than 10—$333.
- At least 10 years, but less than 14—$500.
- At least 14 years, but less than 18—$333.
- 18 years or more—$250.

Dental officers who are colonels in the Army, Air Force, or Marine Corps, or captains in the Navy receive $83 monthly in Variable Special Pay, regardless of their years of creditable service.

Board-Certified Pay: Increasingly, the medical community and ordinary patients expect physicians, dentists, and other health care workers to be board certified. That means they've passed special examinations given for their medical specialty. Board-Certified Pay is the military's special incentive to encourage dentists in uniform to become —and to stay— board certified.

Eligibility: There are two eligibility hoops through which dentists must pass to qualify for Board-Certified Pay. First, they must qualify for Variable Special Pay, which is discussed above. Second, they must be board certified.

The board certifications must come from a body recognized by the American Dental Association. An exception involves dentists in specialties unique to military dentistry for which no formal postgraduate training program exists.

Rates: Here are the monthly rates for Board- Certified Pay that were in effect for 1996. All references to years are based upon the technical meaning of creditable service.

- Less than 12 years—$166.
- At least 12 years, but less than 14—$250.
- 14 years or more—$333.

The rates for Board-Certified Pay don't change every year. In fact, there's no fixed pattern for their improvement.

Additional Special Pay: To persuade military dentists nearing the end of their obligated time in uniform to stay around a little longer, Additional Special Pay provides an extra financial incentive. It offers more additional money to dentists as their time in uniform increases.

Eligibility: Additional Special Pay is available to dentists of the Army, Navy, and Air Force with at least three years of creditable service who sign a formal agreement to stay in the military at least one year more than their current obligations.

Not eligible are interns and people undergoing initial residency training.

Rates: Additional Special Pay is paid in a single, lump-sum amount at the start of each additional 12-month period that a dentist agrees to remain on active duty.

Three amounts were in effect in 1996, depending upon a person's time in service. Eligible dentists could actually qualify for more money than the basic, 12-month payment by committing themselves to 24, 36, or more months in the military.

Here are the rates in effect in 1996:
- At least three years' service, but less than 14—$6,000.
- At least 14 years, but less than 18—$8,000.
- 18 years or more—$10,000.

Dentists who agree to serve more than 12 additional months on active duty receive a single yearly payment at the start of each 12-month period.

These rates, like most of the payments for health care workers, rarely change.

Repayment: Additional Special Pay is an advance payment, and many factors may keep a dentist from serving the length of the obligation. Dentists who leave the military before completing their obligations may have to repay the government unearned payments.

SPECIAL PAY FOR VETERINARIANS AND OPTOMETRISTS

At least one bonus used by the military to encourage physicians and dentists to commit themselves for longer periods of active-duty service is available, in a customized form, to members of other medical specialties.

Called Special Pay for Veterinarians and Optometrists, it gives people in those other health professions an additional financial reason to consider staying longer in uniform.

Eligibility: Usually, people serving on active duty as veterinarians or optometry officers are eligible for this financial incentive if they're already committed to spending one year on active duty, then agree to stay at least one additional year.

Reservists who are veterinarians or optometrists and who are called to active duty for periods of less than one year have been eligible for this additional money if their recalls were to support Operation Desert Storm.

Rates: Participants receive $100 monthly, beginning at the start of the additional active-duty commitment (for active-duty personnel) or on the date of recall (for reservists serving less than a year on active duty).

SPECIAL PAYS FOR NURSES

At least two financial programs are on the books specifically to provide a financial incentive for experienced nurses to join the military and, once aboard, to remain in uniform.

Registered Nurse Accession Bonus: The major bonus program available to nurses is the Registered Nurse Accession Bonus. It's a one-time bonus for qualified nurses as they first enter the military.

Eligibility: Recipients must meet all the professional standards necessary to be registered nurses. Additionally, they must accept commissions in the Nurse Corps of one of the services and agree to serve on active duty at least four years.

Recipients of this bonus who have previously been on active duty must spend at least 12 months in the civilian world before reentering the military to qualify for this bonus.

Ineligible are nurses who received financial help from the Department of Defense to obtain their undergraduate degrees. Also ineligible are people who already hold commissions as Nurse Corps officers.

Amounts: The Registered Nurse Accession Bonus is a one-time, lump-sum payment. The amount may vary, but the maximum is $5,000.

Recoupment: Nurses receive this bonus before the government has received the services for which the military is paying. People who don't fulfill their end of the commitment may have to repay the government for the unearned portion of the bonus.

For Certified Nurse Anesthetists: This group of special, highly trained nurses can receive a lump-sum bonus for each year of additional time in uniform that they agree to serve. Technically, the bonus is known as an incentive special pay.

Eligibility: To be eligible for this financial bonus, nurses must be fully qualified to serve as nurse anesthetists, and they must actually serve in that specialty.

Normally, these specialists must sign formal contracts committing themselves to serve at least 12 months on active duty. Two-year commitments are also possible.

Amounts: The usual rate for this financial incentive is $6,000 per year, although the services can offer smaller amounts. Payment is made in a one-time lump sum at the start of the additional period of active duty.

If a nurse anesthetist signs a formal contract calling for two additional years in uniform, the payments will be made at the yearly lump-sum rate at the start of each 12-month period.

Recoupment: Nurse anesthetists who receive the yearly lump-sum payment must repay the government if they don't serve that entire 12-month period.

PART THREE

LIVING ALLOWANCES

THIRTEEN

OVERSEAS PAYS

In This Chapter:

- *Foreign Duty Pay*
- *Overseas Extension Pay*
- *Family Separation Allowances*

- *Overseas Cost-of-Living Allowance*

When military members stationed overseas face specific hardships, the Pentagon and the Congress have developed programs that balance the financial scales.

This chapter will look at some of them. Details about housing and moving allowances for overseas assignments are detailed in Chapter 14, "Housing Allowances," and Chapter 15, "Moving Pays."

FOREIGN DUTY PAY

Military people in some overseas locations are eligible for a token financial payment for their inconveniences.

> ### Foreign Duty Pay Summary:
>
> Purpose: Token payment for overseas service
> Amounts: $8 to $22.50 monthly (1996)
> Formula: By rank, enlisted only
> Taxable: Yes
> Problem Areas: Sea Pay; not uniform in country.

Foreign Duty Pay is based on a section of a federal law that's officially known as Special Pay While on Duty at Certain Places. Hence, it's sometimes called "Certain Places Pay."

Eligibility: Foreign Duty Pay goes only to enlisted members. Commissioned officers and warrant officers are not eligible.

The "foreign" in Foreign Duty Pay can cover any place outside the 48 contiguous states, plus the District of Columbia. That means that assignments to Alaska, Hawaii, and Puerto Rico have qualified some military members for this addition to the military paycheck.

The word *can* is important. Not all foreign assignments qualify. In fact, not all communities of qualifying countries qualify. Pentagon officials select countries and communities that qualify for foreign duty pay based upon such factors as climate, on-base facilities, and off-base facilities.

Anyone receiving Career Sea Pay is ineligible to receive Foreign Duty Pay for the same period.

Rates: Monthly amounts are based solely on rank. The rates in effect in 1996—in fact, the rates in effect since the program started in 1949—are as follows:

E-1	$ 8.00
E-2	8.00
E-3	9.00
E-4	13.00
E-5	16.00
E-6	20.00

E-7	22.50
E-8	22.50
E-9	22.50

Special Cases: Here's how the rules for Foreign Duty Pay apply to military folks in specific situations.

Court-Martial: Everyone confined while awaiting a court-martial temporarily loses Foreign Duty Pay.

Those acquitted and those whose charges are dismissed receive full Foreign Duty Pay for the total period of their confinement. Those convicted lose Foreign Duty Pay from the first day of their confinements.

Nonjudicial punishments—Article 15s or Captain's Masts—don't affect Foreign Duty Pay.

Hospitalization: For recipients of Foreign Duty Pay hospitalized at a site not approved for Foreign Duty Pay, the extra money ends on the 31st day away from the permanent assignment.

Leave: Recipients of Foreign Duty Pay on leave outside the area designated for that extra money can continue to receive it for the first 30 days. It continues indefinitely for leave taken within the designated area.

Temporary Duty: Foreign Duty Pay is lost on the 31st day of temporary duty outside the designated area. People entering a designated area for temporary duty qualify for Foreign Duty Pay after eight days.

OVERSEAS EXTENSION PAY

Since the early 1980s, the military has been trying to hold down the costs of moving people overseas by offering special bonuses to active-duty people who volunteer to stay longer in a foreign assignment.

This program is commonly called Overseas Extension Pay or Overseas Duty Extension Pay. The official name isn't exactly zippy, for it's formally called Special Pay for Qualified Enlisted Members Extending Duty at Designated Locations Overseas.

Overseas Extension Pay Summary:	
Purpose:	Incentive for longer overseas tours
Amounts:	$80 monthly (1996)
Formula:	None, enlisted only
Taxable:	Yes
Loopholes:	Pick money or extra leave
Problem Areas:	Small program, military picks volunteers.

Eligibility: Overseas Extension Pay goes to enlisted members only. Recipients must:

• Be assigned anywhere *except* the 48 contiguous states and the District of Columbia.

• Possess a skill that their branch of the armed forces wants to keep in that overseas location.

• Sign a contract agreeing to extend the normal overseas tour by one year.

Anyone who's met all these eligibility requirements can choose to receive extra money in the military paycheck. Or that person can decide to pick one of two other options. More about them in the section below entitled "Other Options."

If the government decides to move a recipient of Overseas Extension Pay before the end of that year, the pay continues. If the servicemember chooses to leave early, the extra pay stops.

Rates: Overseas Extension Pay comes in one size. All recipients receive $80 monthly.

Other Options: Everyone who qualifies for Overseas Extension Pay can decline the extra money, picking instead a Rest and Recuperation Absence, more commonly known as "R & R."

R & R is leave time that is not counted against a servicemember's usual 30 days of annual leave. Folks choosing R & R instead of Overseas Extension Pay have two kinds of R & R to pick from: 30 days without free transportation or 15 days that includes free, round-trip government transportation back to the States from the overseas assignment.

Usually, R & R happens between the end of the normal overseas tour and the start of the extra stretch of time overseas. However, commanders have some latitude in delaying R & R periods if someone's absence would interfere with unit readiness.

FAMILY SEPARATION ALLOWANCE

To help pay for the incidental costs of maintaining two households—one for the servicemember overseas, the other for the family in the states—the Pentagon offers additional money in the paycheck called The Family Separation Allowance (FSA).

Family Separation Allowance Summary:

Purpose:	Extra money for extra expenses of separation
Amounts:	Lump-sum $193–$788, or $75 monthly (1996)
Formula:	By BAQ rate or lump-sum
Taxable:	No
Loopholes:	Double payments sometimes possible
Problem Areas:	Confusion over applicable rate; family visits

FSA comes in two different varieties. They're known, succinctly, as Type I and Type II. They're substantially different programs. Type I is the more generous program, but Type II is more common.

General Eligibility: The Family Separation Allowances—

both Type I and Type II—are paid to military members given assignments to new posts where the government won't pay to let their families join them.

If family members move overseas anyway, servicemembers lose FSA if they settle within 50 miles or if the military person lives with them.

Ineligible for FSA are servicemembers whose sole dependents are children in the legal custody of someone else or parents who don't live with the military member.

FSA Type I Eligibility: The rules discussed above under "General Eligibility" apply to recipients of the Family Separation Allowance known as Type I.

The military member must be permanently stationed someplace other than Hawaii, the 48 contiguous states, or the District of Columbia.

> **F**SA Type I = Strictly overseas. Payment based on BAQ.
> FSA Type II = Any unaccompanied assignment. Payment is $75.

Military members must be assigned where government quarters are unavailable.

FSA Type II Eligibility: The rules discussed above under "General Eligibility" apply to recipients of the Family Separation Allowance known as Type II.

The military member must fit into one of three additional categories. Each of these three categories has its own name.

• *FSA-R:* Dependents not authorized government-paid travel to the new assignment.

• *FSA-S:* Member on shipboard duty away from home port for more than 30 continuous days.

• *FSA-T:* Member on temporary duty for more than 30 days, when dependents also don't live near the temporary duty assignment.

Some recipients of Type II Family Separation Allowance may be able to fit into more than one of these three basic categories during a calendar month. Still, they can only receive one month's worth of FSA Type II.

But one double payment is common. If you look again at the definition for FSA-R—"dependents not authorized government-paid travel to new assignment"—you'll realize that fits exactly the definition of everyone receiving Type I Family Separation Allowance. Everyone receiving Type I Family Separation Allowance should also receive the FSA-R kind of Type II allowance.

Rates: The two kinds of Family Separation Allowance— Type I and Type II—have fundamentally different ways of computing payments.

Recipients of the Type I benefits receive their normal Basic Allowance for Quarters, plus an additional BAQ payment each month. The second payment is computed at the without dependents rate.

Recipients of Type II benefits receive a flat rate of $75 monthly (1996). The amount of the Type II payment doesn't change from year to year.

Special Cases: Here's how the rules for Family Separation Allowance affect military people during specific circumstances.

Dual-service couples: When two members of the military are married to each other and have no dependents, both are ineligible for FSA. If they have a child or another family member who qualifies as a dependent, then they can receive FSA during separations, based upon that other dependent.

United Nations: U.S. military personnel on assignment with a United Nations peacekeeping force lose FSA Type I if they receive the U.N.'s "mission per diem."

Visits: Recipients of FSA-Type I and FSA-R continue receiving the extra money during visits by dependents that don't exceed three consecutive months. Recipients of FSA-S and FSA-T lose their extra payments after 30 days.

OVERSEAS COST-OF-LIVING ALLOWANCE

Assignments overseas are a fact of military life. So is the phenomenon of finding oneself with a monthly paycheck that's unable to purchase the same necessities of life overseas that you expect to buy in the States.

Overseas Cost-of-Living Allowance Summary:

Purpose:	Adjustment for lost purchasing power overseas
Amounts:	A few dollars to several hundred monthly
Formula:	Complex, including location, rank, years of service, dependents
Taxable:	No
Loopholes:	Some dependents qualify alone
Problem Areas:	Eating and living in government facilities

To help equalize the loss of purchasing power for other goods and services, servicemembers overseas are commonly entitled to an extra payment called an overseas Cost-of-Living Allowance (COLA).

Eligibility: Active-duty personnel permanently assigned to certain high-cost locations outside the 48 contiguous states are eligible for the Overseas Cost-of-Living Allowance (COLA).

Dependents who are authorized by the military to be overseas can increase the amount of COLA going to a particular servicemember. Dependents can also be eligible for COLA in their own right—that is, when the military member isn't staying at the same location.

Not all countries, or locations within the same country, will qualify servicemembers for the overseas COLA.

Rates: Monthly payments to a given military member depend upon a five-step procedure:

1. Using a chart similar in format to the basic pay chart, determine a servicemember's annual military compensation. There are separate charts for people with dependents and those without families.

2. Take the annual compensation found in step 1 and compare it to a second chart used for spendable income.

3. Get the COLA index number. That's a three-digit number given by the Pentagon for every overseas community. For example, in some communities, the COLA index number is 118. That means expenses exceed typical U.S. expenses by 18 percent.

4. Multiply the COLA index number found in step 3 by the spendable income found in step 2.

5. The figure in step 4 is an annual figure. Divide it by 360 to come up with a daily overseas COLA rate, or by 30 to come up with a monthly rate.

Special Circumstances: Here are some of the typical circumstances in which military families will find themselves that also have an impact on their Overseas COLAs.

Afloat or Afield: COLA recipients living off base who don't have dependents overseas continue receiving their COLAs during deployments expected to last less than 30 days.

For deployments expected to last 30 days or more, COLA payments are reduced to 47 percent of the usual rate. If the deployment ends up lasting less than 30 days, the lost COLA is repaid.

Dependents: Servicemembers with non-command-sponsored dependents overseas who don't eat in government dining facilities are counted as having no dependents in the COLA formula.

If a dependent remains near an old duty station after the servicemember has left—for such things as school or illness—the dependent may be eligible for COLAs for 60 days.

Dependents may also be eligible for COLAs if the active-duty person is being formally confined by civilian or military authorities.

Dual Service: When two people on active duty are married to each other and occupying the same home overseas, each receives 47 percent of the nondependents COLA for any day that person is required to eat in a government dining facility and the full nondependents COLA for every day eating off base.

Foreign Facilities: When food or lodging is provided by a foreign government at no charge to a U.S. military member, the COLA rules treat those foreign items as though they were supplied by the U.S. government, resulting in reduction or elimination of COLA payments.

Jail: COLA recipients without dependents lose it when confined by civilian or military authorities.

Recipients with dependents have their payments lowered when they're confined. The new rate is based on the number of dependents staying in the area of the permanent duty station.

Leave: COLA recipients paid at the without-dependents formula can continue to receive it while on leave. If the leave is taken in the States, COLA can continue for the first 30 days. If the leave is taken overseas, COLA continues for the entire leave period.

FOURTEEN

HOUSING ALLOWANCES

In This Chapter:
- *Variable Housing Allowance*
- *Overseas Housing Allowance*
- *Move-In Housing Allowance*
- *Utility / Recurring Maintenance Allowance*
- *Stateside COLA*

It used to be that everyone in the military got free food, free lodging, and a little spending money from the government. Of course, that was in an era when ground transportation involved horses, sea transport involved sails, and air transport involved the imagination.

Despite improvements in technology, the basic principle has survived. Military people are entitled to more than a paycheck. When the government is unable to provide a roof over the heads of military members and their families, then the government provides extra money so active-duty people can get their own housing.

VARIABLE HOUSING ALLOWANCE

If you live off base in one of the states, the primary addition to your paycheck that can help with housing costs is the Variable Housing Allowance (VHA).

VHA is one of the military's most precisely targeted benefits. Each locality in the United States has its own VHA table. Each one of those tables has a different rate for each rank. And each rank, in turn, has two different rates, one for personnel with dependents, the other for folks without dependents.

Eligibility: Active-duty people living off base in one of the 50 states or the District of Columbia are, generally, eligible for the Variable Housing Allowance.

Surveys by the Defense Department determine which ranks in which communities qualify for VHA payments.

Also eligible for VHA are the following:

• Military members stationed overseas on "unaccompanied tours." Their dependents must live in the States at a place approved for VHA.

• Military members stationed in the States where dependents aren't able to join them. Those dependents also must live in communities approved for VHA.

• Military members living on base in Alaska and Hawaii, when the government won't pay to send dependents to the new assignment and the dependents don't pay their own way to those assignments.

Rates: The Defense Department establishes VHA rates in each stateside civilian community. The rates can range from many hundreds of dollars to a single dollar. The rate may even be zero.

Everyone receiving VHA also receives the Basic Allowance for Quarters (BAQ).

VHA rates are maximums. To get the maximum rate, military folks must be able to show that their actual housing expenses are greater than their VHA plus their BAQ.

Certification: VHA recipients report their housing expenses to their parent service, usually, once a year.

Failure to make that certification can result in the loss of VHA. Falsification of housing costs is taken seriously by the military.

VHA Offset: If VHA plus BAQ is greater than housing costs, the military will withhold some of the VHA that exceeds housing expenses. This ceiling on VHA payments is called the VHA offset.

The offset affects only VHA. Regardless how low your housing costs, you'll always receive full BAQ payments.

VHA Summary:	
Purpose:	Payment for living off base in the States
Amounts:	$1 to $824 monthly (1996)
Formula:	By location, rank, dependents
Loopholes:	Home ownership, inadequate quarters
Problem Areas:	Annual certification, child custody

Two charts are needed to determine whether your housing expenses are affected by the VHA offset. The VHA rate chart is one. The other is called the SU/ME (pronounced "Sue Me") chart. It follows the same format as the rate chart.

SU/ME stands for Standard Utility/Maintenance Expense. It's a listing by rank, area, and dependents for average expenses for electricity, gas, fuel oil, garbage collection, maintenance fees, and a few other typical expenses.

To determine the offset for renters, in one column add these together:

• Your monthly rent.

• Your insurance premium for liability and personal property.

• Your SU/ME number.

In a second column, add these together:

• Your monthly BAQ.

• Your maximum monthly VHA.

Compare the two columns. If the first column (your rental expenses) is larger than the second column (your housing allowances), then you can keep your full VHA payment.

If the second column (your housing allowances) is larger than the first one (your rental expenses), then the military will withhold half the excess in VHA money.

To determine the offset for homeowners, in one column add these together:

• Your monthly mortgage payment.

• Your monthly premium for homeowner's insurance.

• Your monthly amount of real estate taxes.

• Your SU/ME figure.

In a second column, add these together:

• Your monthly BAQ.

• Your maximum monthly VHA.

The mortgage payment can include second mortgages, some home equity loans, and even some personal loans. To count, both home equity loans and personal loans must be used to repair, renovate, or enlarge a residence. Not counted are loans for furnishing homes, decorating homes, or other personal reasons.

Safety Net: Each year, when new VHA rates are issued, many military members see their monthly VHA payments shrink.

Before January 1996, the military offered some financial protection to the *total* paycheck of VHA recipients if a drop in their VHA rates lowered their *total* military income.

Newer rules—retroactive to October 1, 1995—take the complexity out of the VHA safety net. They ensure that your VHA rate can't decrease during a stateside tour if you stay in the same home and pay the same housing costs.

Put another way, the VHA rate in effect when you buy a home or rent an apartment will be the minimum payment throughout your tour. Generally, the rate can go up, but it can't go down.

VHA recipients lose that rate protection if they move into a new home during a stateside tour, or if their actual housing costs decline. Then, they will be vulnerable to the VHA offset if BAQ and VHA are larger than their housing expenses.

VHA and OHA: It's not uncommon for military people with families to receive three housing allowances—BAQ, VHA, and the Overseas Housing Allowance (OHA).

Military folks stationed overseas whose families remain in the States would receive OHA based upon the servicemember's overseas post, VHA at the with-dependents rate appropriate for their stateside home, and BAQ at the with-dependents rate.

Reservists: Reservists called to active duty for less than 20 weeks aren't eligible for VHA. An exception is made for those supporting officially designated "contingency operations."

Reservists ordered to active duty for at least 20 weeks who aren't authorized government-paid transport of their household goods do qualify for VHA. The rate is based upon their civilian home.

Reservists ordered to active duty for at least 20 weeks who do have the military pick up the tab for moving household goods are eligible for VHA based upon the rates at their active-duty location.

Special Circumstances: VHA recipients facing a number of special situations are covered by other provisions within the regulations.

Advance: Military members can request—at the commander's discretion—three months' advance VHA payment, normally to meet unusual move-in costs. Repayment must be made within a year.

Afloat: Usually, folks performing sea duty are governed by the VHA rates in their home-port communities. However, dependents can live in other communities and receive VHA based upon the VHA rates there, if any of these circumstances apply:

• The servicemember will spend an unusually large amount of time at sea.

• The military member is assigned to a ship undergoing overhaul and the government won't pay to move dependents to the site of the shipyard.

• The servicemember is assigned to a ship undergoing overhaul and the government moves the dependents to the vicinity of the naval base where the ship will be stationed after the overhaul.

Alaska and Hawaii: Military folks transferred to Alaska or Hawaii for tours that are officially "unaccompanied" can receive two VHA payments each month—one at the without-dependents level using the appropriate VHA rate for Alaska or Hawaii, and one at the with-dependents level using the appropriate VHA rate for the community in which their dependents live.

These VHA recipients are subject to the VHA offset, discussed above, computing each VHA and each set of housing costs separately.

Death: When military members die on active duty, their survivors may be eligible for VHA at the rate appropriate for their location and rank for 180 days.

If the family was living on base at the time of the servicemember's death, VHA will be paid for 180 days based on the rates in the civilian community to which the family moves.

Divorce: A variety of circumstances have an impact on the VHA payments of divorced servicemembers.

Servicemembers paying child support cannot use in computing the VHA offset any housing expenses for the residence of that child or the former spouse.

A servicemember who is living in government quarters and paying child support is not eligible for VHA. Neither is a servicemember who is stationed overseas and paying child support. A servicemember who is living off base and paying child support is eligible for VHA at the without-dependents rate.

A servicemember with physical custody of a child for at least 90 days, even if that person usually pays child support and the other parent has physical custody, qualifies for VHA at with-dependents rates.

Dual Service: When both husband and wife are on active duty, each qualifies for VHA at the without-dependents level if they have no dependents. If they have a single dependent, both could use the same dependent to qualify for VHA at the with-dependents level.

Hospitalization: VHA continues when a military person is hospitalized. If a VHA recipient is given a permanent-change-of-station move to another hospital, then the servicemember's VHA rate will be based upon the amounts for the vicinity of the new hospital.

Inadequate Quarters: Military people assigned to on-base quarters that are officially declared "inadequate" are not eligible for any VHA payments.

Multiple Homes: When a servicemember lives in one home and family members live in a second, the housing expenses of both homes can be combined for the calculations of the VHA offset.

This happens in stateside tours that are officially "unaccompanied" assignments where off-base housing isn't available, some sea duty, transfers to ships undergoing overhaul, and a few other cases.

Recruits: Eligibility for VHA begins at the same time as eligibility for BAQ. The applicable VHA rates are the ones for the place qualified dependents live.

Shared Residence: Whenever a VHA recipient shares a home with an active-duty spouse or another adult, it affects VHA payments.

Regardless of any private arrangement, the government will treat everyone as paying an equal amount of rent, mortgage payments and routine housing costs. This affects the VHA offset formula discussed above.

OVERSEAS HOUSING ALLOWANCE

If you're living off base outside the United States, the primary addition to your paycheck that can help with housing costs is the Overseas Housing Allowance (OHA).

Like VHA, its stateside counterpart, OHA is tailored to meet the needs of military people and their families who live in specific communities.

OHA is closely associated with two other payments, a Move-In Housing Allowance, and a Utility/Recurring Maintenance Allowance. Since both of those payments go only to OHA recipients, we'll consider them below.

Eligibility: The Overseas Housing Allowance is available to all active-duty people permanently stationed overseas, whether or not they have dependents living with them.

Eligibility includes military folks who are renting homes and buying homes. "Home" can include mobile homes and private vessels.

Ineligible are people living in government-provided quarters and people living in civilian communities without the approval of their commanders. Servicemembers without approval to have family members overseas—so-called non-command-sponsored dependents—are unable to draw OHA at the with-dependents rate.

Rates: The Defense Department has OHA rates for each overseas off-base community where U.S. military people live.

At each location, there is a separate rate for each rank and—within each rank—for those with dependents and those without dependents.

OHA rates are maximums. Deciding how much people will receive in OHA starts with documenting their actual housing expenses. Set that number aside.

Then check the OHA rate for that person's assignment, rank, and dependents. Compare the rate with the actual expense. Take the smaller of the two numbers, and add the Utility/Recurring Maintenance Allowance (discussed below).

From the number that you get from that calculation, subtract the amount of your BAQ or Type-I Family Separation Allowance. What's left after that final subtraction is the amount of OHA that will appear in your monthly paycheck.

If those housing costs are smaller than the OHA rate, then the servicemember receives only as much OHA as needed to cover actual expenses. If housing expenses exceed the OHA rate, then servicemembers must pay the difference.

OHA Summary:

Purpose:	Financial help for costs of living off base overseas
Amounts:	From a couple of dollars to several hundred monthly
Formula:	By location, rank, dependents
Taxable:	No
Loopholes:	Home ownership, inadequate quarters
Problem Areas:	Annual certification, child custody.

Sharing a home with other servicemembers, having a spouse who is in the military or in federal civil service, or buying a home overseas can complicate this equation.

Although OHA rates come in with-dependents and without-dependents levels, the typical OHA rate chart only lists the with-dependents level. For most locations, the without-dependents level is 90 percent of the with-dependents level. OHA rates are subject to review by the military. Normally, they change twice a year. OHA rates are also vulnerable to changes in the value of the dollar. In most cases, OHA is paid in dollars, while contracts with landlords and mortgage companies are paid in the local currency.

Advance: OHA recipients can receive advance payment of their housing allowance. The maximum is one year's OHA and BAQ. Advances must be repaid within a year.

Normally, advances are sought to pay security deposits, advance rent, and other move-in costs. Documentation is required by commanders. Military folks can request an OHA advance at any time: It doesn't have to come at the start of an overseas tour.

Child Support: A servicemember who is assigned to government quarters overseas cannot qualify for OHA solely because that military member is paying child support.

Dual Service: When two military people are married to each other and live together off base in an overseas community, each partner is eligible for OHA. Whether they're buying a home or renting an apartment, the military treats those dual-service couples as though each spouse pays half the housing costs.

Homeownership: In determining OHA payments for homeowners, finance officials will add together the purchase price of the residence and divide it by 120. That's the figure that will be used as the monthly housing cost.

In this case, "purchase price" does not include such things as closing costs, title searches, and other legal fees.

The homeownership formula also applies to OHA recipients who are purchasing a mobile home or a boat, plus monthly lot rental or monthly berthing fees.

Sharers: Each active-duty resident of a home is entitled to receive OHA payments. The government will treat each sharer as paying an equal amount of all housing costs.

Regardless of the number of people living there, each home is eligible for one monthly Utility/Recurring Maintenance Allowance.

MOVE-IN HOUSING ALLOWANCE

The Move-In Housing Allowance (MIHA) comes to the rescue of military folks facing many unforeseen expenses as they try to create a home in a civilian community in a foreign country.

MIHA Summary:	
Purpose:	Making off-base overseas homes livable
Amounts:	Varies; hundreds of dollars common
Formula:	One-time, lump-sum payment
Rates:	By location
Taxable:	No
Loopholes:	Special programs for renters, security
Problem Areas:	Documentation, not all costs covered.

MIHA is actually three programs—MIHA/Miscellaneous, MIHA/Rent, and MIHA/Security. In this section, we'll use the term MIHA to refer to MIHA/Miscellaneous.

Eligibility: Everyone receiving the Overseas Housing Allowance (OHA) is eligible for MIHA. Ineligible are people moving from government quarters to an off-base home after discharge or retirement.

Rates: Each overseas area has a single MIHA rate that covers all servicemembers. Typically, the rates are several hundred dollars. MIHA is a one-time, lump-sum payment that is unaffected by a servicemember's actual move-in costs.

Still, servicemembers must report their actual expenses to the military. This information is used in adjusting MIHA rates for the future.

MIHA Purpose: MIHA/Miscellaneous was created because many civilian homes overseas have, by American standards, stripped interiors. Refrigerators, stoves, cabinets, shelves, screens, light fixtures, and plumbing fixtures are sometimes removed, occasionally even toilets.

Two Other MIHAs: The two other kinds of MIHA available to military folks overseas are reimbursements for actual expenses.

MIHA/Rent: Some one-time expenses facing renters qualify for reimbursement, such as a real estate agent's fees, redecoration fees, and one-time lease taxes.

Not qualifying for reimbursement are advance rental payments, refundable deposits, and recurring costs. Also not qualifying are any one-time expenses related to buying a home.

MIHA/Security: Housing officers or security officers can approve a one-time reimbursement of extraordinary security improvements to a military person's off-base home.

This program exists only in specific countries with terrorism or an unusually high crime rate. Only certain costs are reimbursable. Check before making any purchases.

Special Circumstances: MIHA recipients often find themselves in a variety of common situations that affect this allowance. Here are some of the more typical situations.

Currency Exchange: To determine reimbursements in dollars for MIHA/Rent and MIHA/Security, finance officials use the exchange rate in effect when a servicemember made the purchase.

Homeowners: People purchasing homes overseas who qualify for OHA also qualify for MIHA/Miscellaneous. They can receive MIHA/Security if they meet the proper eligibility rules. But they cannot receive MIHA/Rent.

Multiple MIHAs: People receiving MIHA can receive each of the three versions, so long as they otherwise qualify for them.

Sharers: If you're entitled to MIHA/Miscellaneous, you're entitled to the full amount, even if you share a home with another military member who is paying housing costs and receiving MIHA/Miscellaneous

For MIHA/Rent and MIHA/Security, only one resident of a dwelling can receive the extra money. That person would receive the full amount. The others would receive nothing.

UTILITY/RECURRING MAINTENANCE ALLOWANCE

Most OHA recipients get a second, separate payment in their paychecks called the Utility/Recurring Maintenance Allowance, which is commonly shortened to Utility/Maintenance Allowance.

Like the overall OHA rate, it's customized by overseas location. But unlike OHA, the Utility/Maintenance Allowance has only one basic rate per location for all people living with dependents. Military folks living alone typically receive 75 percent of the local rate.

The Utility/Maintenance Allowance is a maximum. When homes are shared by more than two people, the Utility/Maintenance Allowance takes a proportional cut.

Like the overall OHA rate, amounts for the Utility/Maintenance Allowance are based upon surveys. Normally, rates change once a year.

STATESIDE COLA

Housing costs aren't the only financial expenses that are unequal from one part of the country to another. So are the other expenses that make up a typical household budget, from food and clothing to gasoline and entertainment.

Stateside COLA Summary:	
Purpose:	Payment for living in high-cost U.S. areas
Amounts:	A couple of dollars to a couple hundred
Formula:	By location, dependents
Taxable:	No
Loopholes:	Mobility for dependents
Problem Areas:	Small rates; few qualify.

In 1995, the military began a new program called CONUS COLA—"CONUS" for the standard military shorthand for continental U.S. and "COLA" for Cost-of-Living Allowance.

Eligibility: Three categories of military people are eligible for this extra payment:

• Servicemembers permanently assigned to high-cost areas stateside.

• Military people on permanent, unaccompanied tours overseas, with the "primary dependent" living stateside in a high-cost area.

• Servicemembers stationed permanently in the states, whose primary dependent must live elsewhere in the states in a high-cost area.

This last category involves case-by-case approval by the parent service. Generally, it applies to people assigned to areas with insufficient housing or Navy, Marine, and Coast Guard members facing intense periods afloat.

The references to primary dependent apply to a service-member's spouse or, for an unmarried person, an officially recognized dependent.

Whether a servicemember lives on or off base doesn't affect eligibility for the Stateside COLA.

The second factor affecting eligibility involves the community. Not every high-cost area qualifies a servicemember for the

Stateside COLA. The military picks the areas for which the Stateside COLA will be paid. In 1996, fewer than a hundred communities were approved.

Rates: Two charts are needed to determine an individual's CONUS COLA. One is similar in format to the Basic Pay chart. In 1996, it had rates ranging from $11 for a single E-1 to $45 for an O-10 with dependents.

The other chart is a list of communities designated for CONUS COLA. Beside each community's name is a single number. That's a multiplier. Multiply the multiplier for a given community by the dollar amount appropriate for a service-member's rank and dependents.

More than 90 percent of the multipliers in 1996 were 1. The high was Westchester, New York, with 11.

Only one community's Stateside COLA may be paid to a military person at one time. If a servicemember qualifies for the extra money because of where the dependents live, then the CONUS COLA rate that's paid is the one where the dependents live.

Special Circumstances: Here's how the rules affect military members and their families in a number of specific situations:

Afloat: A vessel's home port is usually the location used to determine whether a servicemember is entitled to the State-side COLA.

Stateside COLA based upon the rates where the dependent lives can be paid to crewmembers of vessels officially listed as performing "unusually arduous" sea duty (which usually means near-continuous sea duty for a year).

Child Support: Servicemembers paying child support and receiving BAQ at the dependent rate (solely because of the child-support payment) or BAQ at the BAQ-Diff rates are eligible for the Stateside COLA at the without-dependents rate.

Dependents: When a servicemember is permanently stationed overseas and the "primary" dependent lives in an officially recognized high-cost area for purposes of the Stateside COLA, the servicemember could receive the extra money set at that community's rate.

A dependent who wasn't living in a high-cost area when the servicemember left for the overseas assignment can move later into a stateside high-cost area and receive the Stateside COLA.

Dual Service: When a husband and wife are both in the military, each one can receive the CONUS COLA, so long as they otherwise qualify. If they have no dependents, each would receive it at the without-dependents level.

If a third person who qualified as a military dependent shared their household, one spouse could collect the Stateside COLA at the with-dependents level and the other would collect it at the without-dependents rate.

Leave: Military personnel on leave are entitled to CONUS COLA, based upon their permanent duty station.

Overseas: When the servicemember is on an unaccompanied tour overseas, the CONUS COLA continues for visits by dependents of less than 90 days.

Overseas COLA: When the service member is on an unaccompanied tour overseas and the family lives in a stateside community that qualifies for the Stateside COLA, the servicemember may receive the Overseas COLA at the without-dependent rate (for the servicemember) and the Stateside COLA at the with-dependents rate (for the dependents).

Reserves: Reservists called to active duty for 20 weeks or more are entitled to the Stateside COLA. Ineligible are reservists called to active duty for less than 20 weeks.

FIFTEEN

MOVING PAYMENTS

In This Chapter:
- *Dislocation Allowance*
- *Temporary Lodging (Stateside—TLE)*
- *Temporary Lodging (Overseas—TLA)*
- *Mileage Allowance and Per Diem (Member)*
- *Mileage Allowance and Per Diem (Dependents)*
- *Government -Paid Transportation*

If the military tells you to pack up your things and move to a place where the government wants you to be, then the least the military can do is pay the costs of moving.

At least, that's the theory. Unfortunately, government studies show that military people end up using money from their own pockets to bear the expense of moving to another assignment. An essential tool to minimize those out-of-pocket costs is a clear, detailed picture of the military programs available to help with moving costs.

DISLOCATION ALLOWANCE

Not every cost associated with moving to a new assignment is covered by allowances, reimbursements, or other financial programs. In fact, military families have to pay some costs from their own pockets.

Dislocation Allowance Summary:	
Purpose:	Financial offset for moving costs
Amounts:	$387 to $1,941 (1996)
Formula:	Lump-sum, twice monthly BAQ rate
Taxable:	No
Loopholes:	Late-arriving families
Problem Areas:	Once per fiscal year.

One financial tool for closing that gap is the Dislocation Allowance, a payment that goes to military families facing a permanent reassignment. It also goes to active-duty folks without dependents, but only under specific conditions.

Eligibility: Receiving orders for a permanent-change-of-station, or PCS, move is the first eligibility requirement for Dislocation Allowance.

With Dependents: Military people with dependents qualify even if the dependents don't go to the new assignment.

Without Dependents: Military people without dependents are entitled to Dislocation Allowance only if not assigned government quarters at their new post.

Assigned is an important word. If the government offers on-base housing and someone declines and moves off base, that person has still been assigned quarters. Such people are ineligible for the Dislocation Allowance.

Evacuation: Any military member stationed overseas who has dependents there who officially qualify as "command-sponsored" is entitled to Dislocation Allowance if the government orders an evacuation of dependents because of international turmoil. In these circumstances, the Dislocation Allowance is also known as the Departure Allowance.

Rates: Dislocation Allowance is based upon the Basic Allowance for Quarters, or BAQ. It's equal to two months' BAQ, no more and no less. The general rule is that military folks can receive only one payment per fiscal year.

An exception involves servicemembers whose families didn't join them at a new assignment. They would have received Dislocation Allowance at the without-dependents rate. If dependents later arrive, a second payment is made, so that both payments equal the Dislocation Allowance at the with-dependents rate.

Special Circumstances: As with any government regulation, a gray area can exist for eligibility and other factors. Here's how the rules affect people in specific situations:

Dual Service: When husband and wife are both on active duty, they live together, and they don't have anyone else living in their family as a dependent, one partner can receive the Dislocation Allowance at the without-dependents rate.

Sea Duty: A servicemember with no dependents in the grade of E-6, or in a higher grade, who's assigned to permanent duty aboard a ship and who decides to live off base instead qualifies for Dislocation Allowance at the without-dependents rate.

TEMPORARY LODGING (STATESIDE—TLE)

Military people moving to new assignments within the states are often eligible for the Temporary Lodging Expense (TLE) to help defray the costs of living in hotels, motels, or other temporary housing.

TLE has an overseas cousin, the Temporary Lodging Allowance (TLA), with which it has more differences than similarities. TLA is discussed later in this chapter.

TLE Summary:	
Purpose:	Financial offset for hotel, motel costs
Amounts:	Maximum $110 daily for 10 days (1996)
Rates:	By actual expenses if less than maximum
Taxable:	No
Loopholes:	Servicemembers and dependents travel separately
Problem Areas:	Not simultaneous with Per Diem; complex formula

Eligibility: Recipients of the Temporary Lodging Expense must be active-duty military members undergoing a permanent-change-of-station (PCS) move in the states.

They must have expenses for temporary lodging not covered by other travel benefits, especially Per Diem. Gaps commonly occur before leaving the old duty station, after reporting to the new duty-station, or when travel takes longer than the official estimate, which is called allowable travel time.

Dependents traveling separately from the active-duty member to a new assignment can qualify for TLE payments.

Not eligible for TLE are people coming on active duty or people leaving active duty.

Rates: The maximum TLE payment is $110 a day. That's not a guaranteed payment. The Temporary Lodging Expense is a reimbursement for very specific expenses.

The actual TLE payment that a servicemember—or family member—will receive is subject to a seven-step formula.

1. Find the per diem rate for the location where you stayed.

2. Multiply that rate by a figure that's based upon the number of people who used the temporary lodging. Those multipliers are:

• 65 percent for the military member.

- 65 percent for a dependent traveling alone.
- 100 percent for a military member and dependent traveling together.
- 100 percent for two dependents traveling together.

Add 25 percent for each additional dependent. It's possible to have a multiplier of more than 100 percent.

3. Multiply the multiplier you got in step 2 by the per diem you discovered in step 1.

4. Multiply the number you got in step 3 by one of two other numbers. Multiply it by 23 percent if the temporary lodging has facilities for preparing your own food and eating. Use 46 percent if the temporary lodging doesn't have such facilities.

5. Add the number you got in step 4 to the actual daily lodging costs. In most cases, that's the amount for room rental.

6. Take the number produced in step 5, making sure you have a *daily* rate, and subtract from it the daily amount of your Basic Allowance for Quarters (BAQ), Basic Allowance for Subsistence (BAS), and if appropriate, Variable Housing Allowance (VHA).

7. Look at the number produced in step 6 and the number produced in step 3. If both numbers are higher than $110, you get the maximum daily TLE rate of $110. If both numbers aren't larger than $110, then your daily TLE payment will be the smaller of the two numbers.

Nonavailability Statement: If temporary government quarters are available at either the old duty station or the new one, active-duty folks must use them. You cannot collect the Temporary Lodging Expense if the on-base guest house has a vacancy.

Nonavailability statements aren't required for temporary lodging between the old and the new assignments.

Duration: For most people, TLE benefits last a maximum of 10 days. Five days is the limit for folks moving from the states to an overseas location.

When qualifying, out-of-pocket expenses were made for more than 10 days (or 5 days for those heading overseas), the servicemember can pick which days' expenses to submit to the TLE formula.

When the servicemembers and family members travel separately on different days, they can combine expenses—for example, the costs of the servicemember's first travel day with a family member's first travel day—for purposes of the TLE formula.

Special Cases: Here are the ways that the regulations governing the TLE affect some special groups of servicemembers:

Dual-Service Couples: When both husband and wife are on active duty, each partner can be entitled to the TLE maximum of $110 a day for 10 days.

One active-duty partner cannot be considered a dependent of the other for the purpose of the TLE formula. If they have dependents, both partners cannot claim the same dependent. Nor can both claim the same expenses.

Friends: If you stay with family or friends while moving to a new assignment, you can't count those days towards the Temporary Lodging Expense, even if you pay them rent.

Per Diem: It's common for active-duty folks to receive both TLE and Per Diem during a PCS move. But they cannot receive TLE and Per Diem for the same day.

Receipts: Keep in mind that the Temporary Lodging Expense is a reimbursement. To get reimbursed you must be able to document your expenses.

TEMPORARY LODGING (OVERSEAS—TLA)

Military members reassigned overseas are frequently eligible for the Temporary Lodging Allowance (TLA) to help defray the costs of living in temporary civilian quarters and eating meals "on the economy."

TLA Summary:	
Purpose:	Eating, lodging costs during overseas moves
Amounts:	Up to 100 percent of expenses
Formula:	By location, size of family, expenses
Taxable:	No
Loopholes:	TLA and TLE during same transfer
Problem Areas:	Reduced with kitchenettes.

As discussed earlier, TLA has a stateside cousin, the Temporary Lodging Expense (TLE), with which it has more differences than similarities.

Eligibility: The Temporary Lodging Allowance goes to active-duty people making a PCS move outside the 48 contiguous states.

Eligible costs involve temporary housing at an overseas location. Many servicemembers will find themselves eligible for the stateside lodging benefit, TLE, at the start of a reassignment and TLA at the overseas conclusion. Or vice versa.

Recipients must receive a written "statement of non-availability" from the local commander to qualify for TLA payments.

Rates: Technically, there's no maximum TLA payment. The amount that any individual will receive is determined by a seven-step formula.

1. Find out the Meals and Incidental Expenses (M&IE) rate—which is a portion of the overall Per Diem rate—for the location where you stayed.

2. Multiply that rate by a figure that's based upon the number of people who used the temporary lodging. Those multipliers are:

• 65 percent for the military member.
• 65 percent for a dependent alone.

• 100 percent for a military member and dependent living together.

• 100 percent for two dependents living together.

Add 25 percent for each additional dependent under 12 and add 35 percent for each additional dependent 12 or older. It's possible to have a multiplier of more than 100 percent.

3. Multiply the multiplier you got in step 2 by the M&IE rate you discovered in step 1.

4. To the number you got in step 3, add the actual daily lodging.

5. From the number you got in step 4, subtract the daily amount of Basic Allowance for Quarters (BAQ) and Basic Allowance for Subsistence (BAS). Set that figure aside for a moment.

6. Find out the overall Per Diem rate for the vicinity where you incurred the temporary lodging expense. Multiply that figure by the percentage calculated in step 2.

7. Compare the figures reached in step 5 and step 6. The government will pay you the smaller figure each day you're qualified for the Temporary Lodging Allowance.

If the temporary lodging has a kitchenette, TLA payments will be reduced. In the formula above, in step 1 and step 6, finance officials will use half the M&IE rate.

Arrival Duration: For most people, the Temporary Lodging Allowance usually lasts no more than 60 days after arrival at a new assignment. Not counted are days spent on temporary duty, on leave away from the new duty station, or in hospitals.

TLA payments for more than 60 days can be approved by local commanders. Usually, extensions are authorized in 10-day periods.

Departure Duration: When military members overseas move out of their permanent quarters, whether government housing or private-sector homes, they're eligible for TLA payments for a maximum of 10 days. Longer periods are possible with a commander's approval.

Special Circumstances: Here's how the rules about TLA affect military members in some common situations:

Friends: If you stay with family or friends while moving to a new assignment, you can't count those days towards the full Temporary Lodging Allowance, even if you pay them rent or make some other financial contribution. However, you would be eligible for partial TLA payments based upon food costs.

Hospitalization: Servicemembers hospitalized while receiving TLA payments may continue receiving the extra money if they're required to keep their temporary housing.

Household Goods: Military folks arriving at an overseas duty station where permanent quarters are ready and the government can provide furniture don't qualify for TLA payments if their household goods haven't arrived.

Late Arrivals: If dependents arrive after the usual 60-day limit has expired, they may be able to qualify for an additional 60 days of TLA benefits, even if the servicemember has already received TLA for 60 days.

When a tour that has been classified as "unaccompanied" has been changed to "accompanied," both the dependents and the servicemember may qualify for TLA payments.

Leave: Payment of the Temporary Lodging Allowance ends when a servicemember goes on leave away from the vicinity of the permanent duty station. It can resume when the servicemember returns, so long as other eligibility rules are met.

Continuing to receive TLA payment on leave are servicemembers who take leave in the vicinity of their duty stations and those with at least one dependent who qualifies for TLA money remaining near the permanent duty station.

New Dependents: Servicemembers who acquire dependents while stationed overseas (e.g., through marriage or the birth of a child) can't receive TLA payments when the new dependents arrive overseas. However, at the end of that assignment, those military families can receive end-of-tour TLA payments.

Per Diem: It's common for active-duty folks to receive both TLA and Per Diem while making a PCS move. But they cannot receive TLA and Per Diem for the same day.

Receipts: Keep in mind that the Temporary Lodging Allowance is, essentially, a reimbursement. To get reimbursed you must be able to document your expenses.

Renovations: Residents of government quarters overseas who are unable to prepare meals at home because of renovations become eligible for partial TLA payments to reimburse them for the costs of eating out.

Sea-Duty: Servicemembers receiving Per Diem while awaiting the arrival of a ship at a new home port can receive TLA benefits on behalf of their dependents.

Servicemembers leaving their ship before it returns to home port in order to make PCS moves may be authorized to receive TLA payments. They cannot receive TLA and Per Diem for the same days, but it's possible for Per Diem recipients to receive TLA payments based upon the temporary lodging costs of their dependents.

Temporary Duty: Full TLA benefits are available to some servicemembers with orders for temporary duty expected to last at least 90 days. Recipients must be without dependents at the duty station. And they must have vacated their permanent quarters before going on temporary duty.

TLA benefits only apply to these folks for the period after the end of their temporary-duty assignment, not for any period before going on temporary duty.

MILEAGE ALLOWANCE AND PER DIEM (MEMBER)

Most members of the U.S. military own cars. When they're given PCS orders, their household goods may get to the new assignment on a moving van, but the servicemember, spouse, and other dependents get to their new home in the family car.

The government benefit that pays for the servicemember to drive to new assignments is called MALT-Plus. That stands for Monetary Allowance in Lieu of Transportation. It's called "Plus" because it frequently includes a Per Diem.

Eligibility: Active-duty members who are reassigned to new installations are usually entitled to a mileage allowance to cover costs of getting the family car to the new duty station, plus a so-called flat-rate Per Diem to help pay for food.

Mileage Rates: Two major factors control the amounts for the mileage allowance—the distance traveled and the number of people traveling together.

Distances aren't the actual number of miles logged on a car's odometer. The government has charts with official distances between major points in the United States.

The other major factor is the number of people traveling together. In this case, a "traveler" can be the servicemember, dependents traveling alone, or the servicemember traveling with dependents. Those rates per mile in 1996 are 15 cents for one traveler, 17 cents for two travelers, 19 cents for three travelers, and 20 cents for four or more travelers.

Per Diem Rates: If you're entitled to a per-mile allowance during a PCS move, then you're also entitled to a Per Diem of $50 daily (1996).

It's a flat rate. It isn't affected by actual costs. But split hairs can be found in defining "day." For folks with PCS orders, the official day falls into four quarters:

- One minute past midnight to 6 A.M.
- 6:01 A.M. to noon.
- One minute past noon to 6 P.M.
- 6:01 P.M. to midnight.

You get $12.50 of Per Diem per quarter-day. The clock

starts when you leave your old duty station and ends when you arrive in your new one. Essentially, the Per Diem "clock" stops while travelers are on leave.

Allowable Travel Time: In addition to the four quarters of the "Per Diem day," another important element of time for military folks undergoing a PCS move is "allowable travel time."

	Mileage Allowance and Per Diem (Member) Summary:
Purpose:	Offset costs of family car during transfers
Amounts:	15 cents per mile, $50 per day (1996)
Rates:	By mile, days, number of occupants
Taxable:	No
Loopholes:	Servicemembers and dependents travel separately.

Essentially, this is a way of using distance to measure time. Officially, a travel day is 350 miles. If you travel a distance that's a multiple of 350—such as 700 miles, or 1,050, or 1,400—you become eligible for another day of Per Diem after covering at least 176 more miles.

On the first day's travel, one day's Per Diem is authorized for distances of 525 miles or less. Military folks must go at least 526 miles to qualify for a second day's Per Diem at the start of a move.

Special Circumstances: Here are some of the more common kinds of situations that require an understanding of finer points in the regulations:

Divided Homes: If family members don't go to a new duty station with the servicemember, the servicemember can be entitled to the mileage allowance and flat-rate Per Diem if he or she accompanies the families from the old duty station to the family's new home, and from there to the new duty station. This kind of trip must be approved in advance by the official who issued the PCS orders.

Discharges: For most people discharged from the armed forces, their move to the civilian world is treated as a PCS move. The same mileage allowance and flat-rate Per Diem are paid. (See chapter 17, "Discharge Pay", for more details.)

Dual Service Couples: When husband and wife are both on active duty and traveling together to the same new assignment, each is entitled to a Per Diem of $50 daily (1996). Only one, however, can claim the mileage allowance based upon the distance they traveled.

This is also the rule when the people traveling together are on active duty but they aren't married. Each gets a Per Diem; one gets the mileage allowance.

Leave: Many military members go on leave during transfers. Their mileage allowance is based on official distances, and their Per Diem is based on "allowable travel time."

Sea Duty: When a ship changes home port, crew members who accompany the ship to the new home port may be entitled to mileage allowance and the flat-rate Per Diem to return to the old home port to pack and move. They'd also be eligible for mileage allowance and the flat-rate Per Diem to travel from the old home port to the new one.

Tolls: Recipients of the mileage allowance can be reimbursed for tolls, ferry fares, and similar costs.

MILEAGE ALLOWANCE AND PER DIEM (DEPENDENTS)
In basic design and in many details, the financial benefits for dependents during PCS moves are the same as the mileage allowance and Per Diem for active-duty military personnel.

Although these payments are paid because dependents—
without a servicemember—made certain kinds of travel and
the dependents are said to have earned the reimbursements in
their own right, all payments are made to the military member
and none are made to the dependent.

Eligibility: If a military member receives orders to make a
PCS move and uses a privately owned vehicle, that person's official dependents frequently qualify for a mileage allowance
and Per Diem for their travel.

Dependents don't have to travel with the servicemember to
qualify. Ineligible are family members who aren't official "dependents" or who aren't moving to the new assignment.

Mileage Rates: See "Mileage Rates" above under "Mileage
Allowance and Per Diem (Member)."

Per Diem Rates: When dependents travel to a new assignment with the active-duty member, each dependent 12
years of age and older is entitled to $37.50 daily. For depen-
dents younger than 12, the rate is $25 daily.

Mileage Allowance and
Per Diem (Dependents) Summary:

Purpose:	Offset car costs and meals during transfers
Amounts:	15 cents per mile, $50 per day (1996)
Rates:	By mile, days, number of occupants
Taxable:	No
Loopholes:	Two vehicles, unaccompanied tours.

When two or more dependents travel together to a new
assignment without the servicemember, one dependent is entitled to $50 daily, while each additional dependent would
receive $37.50 or $25 daily, depending on whether those dependents were 12 or older.

If a military family is traveling to a new assignment in two or more cars at the same time, the dependents are considered to be traveling *with* the military member,

Like the servicemember's Per Diem, the amount received by dependents is a flat-rate payment unaffected by actual expenses.

Vehicles: If your service has authorized travel to a new assignment by private car—officially known as a "privately owned conveyance" (POC)—usually you're automatically entitled to use two family vehicles.

A husband and wife traveling in one car are entitled to 17 cents per mile. In two cars, each is entitled to the one-traveler rate of 15 cents per mile, for a family total of 30 cents per mile in two cars.

Using three or more family cars requires the permission of the official who issued the reassignment orders.

Unaccompanied Tours: When military members serve unaccompanied tours overseas, their dependents are entitled to receive the regular mileage allowance and Per Diem as they travel to anywhere in the United States where they intend to make their home.

Or, if the servicemember will be stationed at another overseas location following the unaccompanied tour, the government will pay for the family to travel to that second site when the servicemember goes to the first one.

These moves are known as "designated places" moves. That's because the servicemember designates the place to which the family will move.

Special Circumstances: Here's how the rules for dependent travel affect special groups of people:

Divorce: When a military member acquires legal custody of a child, the government will authorize regular dependent travel benefits so the child may join the active-duty parent.

Late Approval: When a military person goes overseas with PCS orders that don't permit government-paid travel for family members, those dependents can receive regular government travel benefits if the services later approve dependents at the new duty station.

Overage Dependents: Unless they're handicapped, the children of military members officially cease being dependents at age 23 for students and 21 for nonstudents.

If a dependent child crosses that threshold into nondependency while the servicemember is overseas, the government will grant regular dependent travel benefits to that person when the military member receives the next set of PCS orders.

Reserves: Reservists and National Guardsmen on extended active duty are entitled to the same travel benefits for their family members as the rest of the armed forces.

Sea Duty: Usually, when a military member is ordered to sea duty, family members are entitled to the regular travel benefits when they move to the new home port.

When the sea duty is officially labeled as "unusually arduous" or the vessel is scheduled to operate outside the United States for at least one year, family members qualify for the mileage allowance and Per Diem to move to any location in the 48 contiguous states.

GOVERNMENT-PAID TRANSPORTATION

When PCS orders have made a servicemember or family members eligible for government-paid airline tickets, train tickets, bus tickets, or passenger liner tickets, some other travel-related expenses can be reimbursed by the military.

Servicemembers and family members traveling by family car from home to the airline terminal, bus station, or other point of departure, can receive the mileage allowance for the distance between home and the terminal. The "clock" for per diem starts when they leave home.

Reimbursable expenses include the following:

• Public transportation needed to get to the government-provided transportation. That includes taxis, buses, and streetcars and applies only when free transportation is unavailable.

• Tips to train attendants. Limit of $1 per day.

• Tips to taxi drivers. Limit of 15 percent of fare.

• Costs of obtaining passports, passport photos, birth certificates, and visas.

• Costs of traveler's checks.

• Tips to stewards aboard ship. Not to exceed $5 per day for one traveler, $9 for two, $13 for three, $16 for four.

Two rules are always good to remember: First, when expenses for a single item exceed $25, the government cannot reimburse you if you don't have receipts.

Second, talk to the folks at the travel office before you incur any large expenses under the assumption that the government will pay you back.

SIXTEEN

LINE-OF-DUTY PAYMENTS

If the government requires that military members do somthing they wouldn't ordinarily do, then the government should ensure that the folks on active duty are reimbursed for any expenses that flow from that order. At least, that's the theory.

This chapter has assembled details about a variety of disparate payments. None of the programs appear in any official publication as "Line-of-Duty Payments." That phrase is being used here for the convenience of new members of the military who are still learning the ropes—and the language.

TEMPORARY-DUTY FOOD AND LODGING

Military members who are sent overnight on government business away from home usually qualify for financial help from the military in paying for their food and lodging.

Lodging-Plus Summary:	
Purpose:	Financial help on TDY/TAD
Amounts:	Widely varies
Rates:	By location, actual lodging costs
Taxable:	No
Loopholes:	Home purchases, mobile homes
Problem Areas:	Lodging or food provided; partial days

Called Lodging-Plus, it reimburses military travelers for the costs of getting a hotel room or other temporary lodging. The "plus" is that it also provides a Per Diem, or small amount for meals.

Eligibility: Servicemembers performing temporary duty (TDY) or temporary additional duty (TAD) are eligible for Lodging-Plus when their orders clearly authorize the payments.

Lodging Rates: The lodging portion of Lodging-Plus is, essentially, a reimbursement to a military member for the costs of renting a room in a hotel or another commercial establishment.

The reimbursement isn't for an unlimited amount, however. The government sets maximum payments for each community, based upon local costs.

Rates have been established for hundreds of localities, both stateside and overseas. Stateside civilian communities catering to tourists may have two rates—one for peak tourist season, another for the rest of the year.

Recipients of Lodging-Plus can stay in on-base guest houses, BOQs, and BEQs. Their expenses for those government quarters will be treated the same as expenses incurred in off-base hotels. If facilities are available on base for a particular night, servicemembers can be denied reimbursement for any off-base lodging for that night.

Per Diem Rate: Recipients of Lodging-Plus also receive a Per Diem to help pay for their meals. Technically, these are known as Meals and Incidental Expenses, or M&IE, rates.

M&IE rates are set by the government for each locality. They're not reimbursements. Everyone gets the maximum M&IE rate for each locality. Stateside, M&IE came in four sizes in 1996. The daily rates are:

- $26.
- $30.
- $34.
- $38.

Overseas, the M&IE rates fluctuate significantly, going from a low of $13 daily in many places to more than $200 daily in many parts of Japan.

The day someone goes on temporary duty and the day that person returns are each divided into four quarters. For the day of departure and the day of arrival, you get one-fourth of Per Diem per quarter-day. Those quarter-days are:

- One minute past midnight to 6 A.M.
- 6:01 A.M. to noon.
- One minute past noon to 6 P.M.
- 6:01 P.M. to midnight.

M&IE payments are reduced if food has been provided in a military dining facility or by a school, conference, or commercial vessel for which the government had paid costs that include the price of meals.

Folks who lose the meals portion of M&IE are still eligible for the incidental-expenses portion of their Per Diem. It equals $2 daily in the United States and $3.50 daily overseas (1996).

Special Circumstances: Here are some other provisions

in the rules that affect servicemembers and their families in narrowly drawn—but commonly experienced—situations.

Double Occupancy: When a servicemember drawing Lodging-Plus shares a room with another military member or U.S. government employee, that military member will be credited with paying one-half the double-occupancy rate, regardless of actual expenses.

When the roommate is not a military member or U.S. government employee, the government will use the single-occupancy rate at that establishment for the Lodging-Plus formula.

Double-Rent: If a military member ends up paying for lodging at two places on the same day, the services will consider the room that was occupied at—or closest to—midnight as the expense used to compute the lodging-portion of Lodging-Plus.

Total payment for both rooms is still limited to the local lodging cap for the community where the servicemember stayed at—or closest to—midnight.

Friends: Recipients of Lodging-Plus who stay with family or friends are ineligible for the lodging portion of the program, even if they pay their hosts for the room. They are still eligible for the M&IE portion of the Lodging-Plus program.

Houses: Military folks receiving Lodging-Plus can continue to receive the payment if they stay in a rented house or apartment.

The expenses that can be used to compute the lodging portion of the payment include rent of the unit; rent of such necessary furniture and appliances as stoves, beds, tables, chairs, refrigerators, and vacuum cleaners; and utilities, including connection and disconnection fees.

Mobile Homes: Military members on temporary duty who rent or own mobile homes and recreational vehicles can continue to receive Lodging-Plus if they live in those vehicles.

Expenses that will be used to compute the lodging portion

of the payment include vehicle rental, rental fees for parking spaces, dumping fees, and shower fees.

Purchases: Active-duty members who purchase a home while on temporary duty at the temporary-duty assignment retain their eligibility for Lodging-Plus. Expenses counted in the formula for the lodging portion of this benefit include interest payments (but not payments on the principal), monthly property tax, and monthly utility costs (but not hook-up or installation charges).

Temporary Lodging Allowance (TLA): When recipients of Lodging-Plus are sharing a temporary home with family members who are receiving the Temporary Lodging Allowance (TLA), the servicemember will be credited with paying half the lodging expenses, regardless of how many family members are present.

VIP ESCORT
Not even the U.S. military is able to write enough rules to cover every situation. The unexpected occurs with expected frequency.

Actual Expense Allowance Summary:	
Purpose:	Financial help for extraordinary TDY/TAD expenses
Amounts:	Full food, lodging costs
Formula:	Case by case
Taxable:	No
Loopholes:	Home purchases, mobile homes
Problem Areas:	Rarely authorized.

When it comes to extraordinary expenses for servicemembers traveling on government business, especially those escorting VIPs, a little-known program that may be of service is called the Actual Expense Allowance. This is a rare, tightly controlled benefit.

Eligibility: Servicemembers performing temporary duty or temporary additional duty to escort dignitaries, attend major national and international celebrations, or serve at natural disasters can qualify.

Rates: The Actual Expense Allowance is a reimbursement with several different maximum payments, depending upon circumstances. The rates can range from 150 percent to 300 percent of the daily Lodging-Plus rate (discussed above under "Temporary-Duty Food and Lodging").

Special Circumstances: Here are some ways the rules for the Actual Expense Allowance handle some very specific kinds of problems.

Air-Crews: The men and women who fly dignitaries generally don't qualify for the Actual Expense Allowance.

Lodging-Plus: Meals and incidental expenses may be reimbursed under the Lodging-Plus program (discussed in the section above, "Temporary-Duty Food and Lodging"), while lodging expenses are covered by the Actual Expense Allowance.

Government Quarters: When recipients of the Actual Expense Allowance stay in U.S. government quarters, they can receive $2 daily for incidental expenses in the States, or $3.50 daily overseas.

UNIFORM ALLOWANCES

Food and lodging are only two-thirds of the basic services that military members in modern times have expected their government to provide, free of charge, in return for their services. The third element is clothing.

Either the government gives active-duty personnel the military uniforms, or the government provides money for service-members to purchase their own. Here are the rates in effect in 1996 to help military personnel purchase their uniforms.

Officer Rates: Officers are entitled to a one-time Initial Uniform Allowance payment of $200.

The payment is made upon commissioning in a Regular component, upon first reporting to active duty for a non training period of more than 90 days, or upon completing 14 days' active-duty training as a member of a reserve component.

Enlisted Programs: Enlisted members of the military, at different times during their active-duty careers, may receive three different payments from the government to help them buy uniforms.

They are the Initial Clothing Allowance, the Basic Replacement Allowance and the Standard Replacement Allowance. The size of each allowance changes yearly to keep pace with the actual costs of purchasing a typical clothing bag of uniform items.

Here are the rates in effect for 1996:

	Initial	Basic	Standard
Army			
Men	$958	$194	$277
Women	1,171	234	335
Navy			
Men	894	205	291
Women	1,269	259	371
Air Force			
Men	829	173	248
Women	1,018	219	313
Marine Corps			
Men	923	216	309
Women	1,147	198	284

These amounts usually change every year, with the new rates taking effect with the start of the new federal fiscal year on October 1.

Initial Clothing Allowance: Technically, enlisted personnel are eligible for the Initial Clothing Allowance at the start of their first enlistments. Practically, most first-termers won't see any money. Instead, they'll be given the uniform items that the allowance is designed to pay for.

Two other groups of people are likely to receive money:

• Former enlisted people coming back on active duty after spending more than three months as civilians.

• Reservists who haven't been on active duty for at least three months who are scheduled to be on active duty for at least six months.

Basic Replacement Allowance: Enlisted members with three years or less on active duty are eligible for the Basic Replacement Allowance. The money is to replace items expected to last less than three years. This allowance is paid once each year.

Standard Replacement Allowance: Enlisted members with more than three years on active duty are eligible for the Standard Replacement Allowance. The money helps servicemembers purchase items expected to require replacement after three years. This allowance is also paid once each year.

Women-Only Allowances: Although each category of uniform allowances have separate rates for female servicemembers, there's a special kind of allowance that's available to women only.

Called the Initial Cash Allowance, it's designed to permit military women to purchase underclothing after they first come on active duty. The allowance is for enlisted women only.

Navy Programs: Several uniform allowances are unique to the Navy.

Reserve Allowance: Called Partial Clothing Allowance, this payment is for reservists called to extended active duty in the ranks of E-1 to E-6. The 1996 rates provided $162 for men and $282 for women.

Chief Petty Officers: This one-time allowance of $720 (1996) is given for purchase of uniform items unique to E-7s, and is payable on promotion. In addition, a replacement allowance of $44 is paid annually (1996) to maintain this stock of uniform items.

Special Initial Clothing Allowance: This allowance is provided to enlisted sailors required to wear individual uniform items not included in either the Initial Clothing Allowance or the Partial Clothing Allowance, especially officer candidates, aviation officer candidates, and naval aviation cadets. The 1996 rates were $1,330 for women and $1,017 for men.

CIVILIAN CLOTHING ALLOWANCE

For some military folks, the uniform of the day isn't a uniform. Military members in certain fields—intelligence and criminal investigations, for example—or in certain foreign areas where the presence of the U.S. military is unwelcome can be authorized a special allowance to pay for civilian clothing to wear during duty hours.

Civilian Clothing Allowance Summary:	
Purpose:	Active-duty job calls for civilian dress
Amounts:	One-time payment of $240 to $1,127 (1996)
Rates:	By season, temporary duty
Taxable:	No
Loopholes:	Temporary duty; consecutive tours, extensions
Problem Areas:	No extra payment for women; rates low

The Civilian Clothing Allowance is a rarity, with the services tightly controlling who gets them and under what circumstances. Slightly more than 5,000 military members qualify during a single year.

Eligibility: When the performance of official duties regularly requires military personnel to wear civilian dress, the services have the authority to approve payment of a Civilian Clothing Allowance. Typically affected are military members assigned to embassies overseas, plus some intelligence and law-enforcement personnel. Approval is almost on a case-by-case basis.

Officers are only eligible for this allowance when stationed overseas.

Recipients of the Civilian Clothing Allowance may be eligible for extra payments if the assignment for which they receive the extra payment is lengthened.

Military members on temporary duty and temporary additional duty can become eligible for these payments if their temporary-duty assignment requires them to wear civilian clothes on the job.

Initial Payments: The amount of the Civilian Clothing Allowance is determined by two factors—the length of the tour for which civilian clothing is needed and whether the servicemember will need separate sets of clothing for winter and summer.

Here are the rates in effect in 1996, based upon tour length and seasonal changes of clothes:

	Winter and Summer	**One Season**
Under 12 Months	$721	$482
12–24 Months	962	632
Over 24 Months	1,217	787

When a servicemember is given temporary-duty orders that require wearing civilian clothes to perform military duties, a Civilian Clothing Allowance can be authorized. The temporary duty must last at least 15 days. When the temporary assignment is less than 30 days, the payment under 1996 rates is $240. When the temporary-duty assignment is scheduled to last 30 days or more, the payment is $449.

Follow-On Payments: When tour extensions or back-to-back tours happen, military members are entitled to an extra payment of the Civilian Clothing Allowance. Those payments are computed as a percentage of the Civilian Clothing Allowance then in effect (not the rate the servicemember originally received).

Here are the rates for those follow-on payments:

• Additional six months in assignment, 20 percent.
• Additional 12 months in assignment, 30 percent.
• Full, additional tour, 50 percent.

PART FOUR

SPECIAL TIMES, SPECIAL CASES

SEVENTEEN

DISCHARGE PAYS

Everyone came from someplace. When members of the military approach the end of their time on active duty, they find themselves confronting an array of programs, benefits, and payments designed to ease their return home.

Since this is *The Military "Money" Guide,* our focus will be upon the programs that put—or directly translate into—money in the pockets of folks leaving the armed forces. But we'll touch upon some of the programs and benefits that have a financial impact upon soon-to-be veterans.

NORMAL DISCHARGES

For the vast majority of the 200,000-plus people who leave the military every year, the process of returning to the civilian world is fairly straightforward. They settle their accounts with the armed forces, receive a last paycheck, and hit the road. Here are the major factors affecting a servicemember's final check from the military, and a few factors that continue into one's civilian days.

Final Paycheck: Military people are entitled to the full range of active-duty pay, allowances, and benefits until the last minute of the last day that they're technically on active duty.

For military members normally paid electronically, that's how their last paycheck will be paid unless they make provisions in advance with their local finance officers for a payment by check or in cash.

Taxes are usually deducted from the final military paycheck, as are any sums owed the government.

Cashing-in Leave: Military personnel who have not used all of their leave before their discharge date can cash-in any unused leave.

Each day of unused leave is equal to one-thirtieth of the servicemember's Basic Pay, using rates in effect on the last active-duty day. No other kinds of pay are considered for cashing in leave.

Leave earned in a combat zone subject to tax protection is free of taxes when it's cashed in.

Government-Paid Transportation: As far as the military is concerned, a servicemember returning home after being discharged from active duty is making a PCS move. (See chapter 15, "Moving Payments," for details.)

Health Insurance: The military offers transitional health insurance for servicemembers being discharged.

If you want it, you must apply for it before your discharge

date. It isn't free. To be covered, you must pay premiums. In 1996, the premiums for a three-month period were about $400 for individuals and about $900 for families.

Recipients of Separation Pay, VSI, and SSB are eligible for medical care in on-base facilities and under CHAMPUS for up to 120 days after their discharges. Some exit bonus recipients have a shorter post-discharge period of coverage.

Unemployment Compensation: Most people leaving active duty are eligible for unemployment compensation. That's a government-run program that provides a minimum income to workers who are between jobs.

Twenty-six weeks is the longest that anyone can receive unemployment compensation. Rates vary from state to state. In 1996, the average weekly payment for unemployment compensation was slightly more than $200 per week.

Veterans coming off active duty can file for unemployment compensation in any state. It doesn't have to be the state of the last assignment, the state where you grew up, or even a state in which you ever lived.

SEPARATION PAY

Separation Pay is a one-time, lump-sum payment given by the government to midcareer military people with good records who have been involuntarily selected for discharge, usually to meet manpower goals within their specialties.

Like the other major exit bonuses—the Special Separation Benefit (SSB) and the Voluntary Separation Incentive (VSI)—Separation Pay isn't a benefit to which anyone has a formal right. It's a management tool.

Eligibility: Separation Pay applies to members of the active-duty military, both officers and enlisted members. It can apply, with slightly different rules, to members of the reserves and National Guard who are on extended active duty.

Separation Pay Summary:

Purpose:	Compensation for involuntary end of careers
Formula:	One-time payment based on Basic Pay, years of service
Rates:	Varies widely
Taxable:	Yes, fully
Loopholes:	Sometimes offered to people who decline SSB and VSI
Problem Areas:	Not always offered to everyone who declines SSB and VSI; heavy tax burden.

The military decides who will be given Separation Pay. Federal law requires these candidates to pass through each of four specific eligibility hoops:

• The candidate must have served at least six years—but less than 20—on active duty.

• The discharge papers must describe the member's service as "honorable."

• Reenlistment (enlisted members) or continuation (officers) must have been denied for reasons unrelated to their job performance.

• The discharged servicemember must agree to spend three years in the reserves.

Sometimes, a clearer view of eligibility involves a look at the rules for ineligibility. The following groups of servicemembers are *not* eligible for Separation Pay:

• Those who decline training.

• Those who request discharge.

• Those discharged before the end of the initial obligation.

• Those eligible for retired pay.

• Those whose discharge was ordered by court-martial.

• Those discharged under "other than honorable" conditions.

• Those discharged for unsatisfactory or substandard performance.

"Half-Pay" Eligibility: Separation Pay is unique in that some people who are otherwise ineligible can receive a reduced version known as Half-Separation Pay.

Eligibility for Half-Separation Pay applies to people who don't fit into any of the "ineligible" categories discussed above.

It can go to people who are officially rated as "not fully qualified for retention," who are denied reenlistment or continuation, and who fall into one of the following categories:

• They've reached their expiration of obligation.

• They are discharged "for convenience of government."

• They failed drug or alcohol rehabilitation.

• They are discharged for security reasons.

• They failed a weight-control program.

Although honorable discharges are needed for full Separation Pay, the half version can go to people with general discharges.

Rates: Separation Pay is a one-time, lump-sum bonus given to military members during their last day on active duty. It is fully taxable.

A simple three-step formula is used to compute an individual's payment for Separation Pay:

1. Multiply the last monthly Basic Pay by 12.

2. Multiply that figure by 10 percent.

3. Multiply that figure by the number of years on active duty.

Note that only Basic Pay is used in this equation. For determining the number of active-duty years, partial years are rounded to the nearest month and only full months are counted.

For people receiving Half-Separation Pay, the same formula applies with an extra, final step. That final step calls for dividing the figure achieved by the regular Separation Pay formula in half.

Other Rules: Separation Pay recipients who later qualify for military retired pay will have the full amount of their Separation Pay deducted from their retirement checks. Most recipients who later qualify for VA disability compensation will lose $1 of VA money for every dollar of Separation Pay they received.

SPECIAL SEPARATION BENEFIT (SSB)

The Special Separation Benefit (SSB) is one of several bonuses offered by the government to some military members as an incentive to persuade them to leave active duty.

SSB Summary:

Purpose:	Financial persuasion to leave active duty
Formula:	One-time payment based on rank, years of service
Rates:	Varies widely
Taxable:	Yes, fully
Loopholes:	Recipients choose between SSB and VSI
Problem Areas:	One-time offer; heavy tax burden

Like the other major exit bonuses—Separation Pay and the Voluntary Separation Incentive (VSI)—the military sees SSB as a management tool to reduce the number of people in uniform as painlessly as possible. It's not a right; it doesn't automatically go to anyone.

Eligibility: Active-duty personnel, including reservists and National Guardsmen on extended active duty, can receive SSB.

Would-be SSB recipients are identified by the military, usually by skill, rank, and year group. Those people have the option of choosing SSB, choosing the VSI companion benefit, or deciding to take their chances by remaining longer on active duty.

Some people who decline SSB may find themselves discharged against their wishes from the military with the less-generous Separation Pay—or with no exit bonus at all.

Recipients must agree to spend at least three years in the reserves.

Rates: SSB is a one-time, lump-sum payment given to eligible military members on their last day on active duty. The bonus is fully taxable.

A simple three-step formula is used to calculate the amount of a SSB payment:

1. Multiply the person's last monthly Basic Pay by 12.

2. Multiply that figure by the number of active-duty years.

3. Take that figure and multiply it by 15 percent.

Note that only Basic Pay is included in the formula.

Other Rules: SSB recipients who leave the reserves for any reason other than a medical disability before the end of their three-year obligation must repay the government for the entire bonus.

SSB recipients who later serve on active duty can keep their SSB payments and also their full military paychecks.

Recipients who later qualify for military retired pay will have the full amount of their SSB payment deducted from their retirement checks. SSB recipients who later qualify for VA disability compensation will lose $1 of VA money for every dollar of SSB they received.

VOLUNTARY SEPARATION INCENTIVE (VSI)

The Voluntary Separation Incentive (VSI) is the discharge benefit that keeps on giving. Recipients receive a substantial check during their last day on active duty, followed by annual payments from the government for many years.

VSI Summary:	
Purpose:	Financial persuasion to leave active duty
Formula:	Annual payments, based on rank, years of service
Rates:	Varies widely
Taxable:	Yes
Loopholes:	Recipients choose between VSI and SSB
Problem Areas:	Reserve commitment; one-time offer

Despite the name, VSI isn't strictly a "voluntary" program. Like the other major exit bonuses—Separation Pay and the Special Separation Benefit (SSB)—the military sees it as a management tool to reduce the number of people in uniform as painlessly as possible.

Eligibility: Active-duty personnel, including reservists and National Guardsmen on extended active duty, can receive VSI.

Would-be VSI recipients are identified by the military, usually by skill, rank, and year group. Those people have the option of choosing VSI, choosing the SSB companion benefit, or deciding to take their chances by remaining longer on active duty.

Some people who decline VSI may find themselves discharged against their wishes from the military with the less-generous Separation Pay, or with no exit bonus at all.

Rates: VSI is paid in installments, with the first payment made on a servicemember's last day in the military. Payments continue on the anniversary date of the veteran's discharge.

VSI payments continue for twice as long as a person served on active duty. Put another way, for each year of active-duty service, recipients get VSI for two years.

A simple two-step formula is used to calculate the amount of the annual VSI payments:

1. Multiply the person's last monthly Basic Pay by 12.
2. Take that figure and multiply it by 2.5 percent.

Note that only Basic Pay is included in the formula. Also note that there's no mechanism for giving annual cost-of-living adjustments (COLAs) to VSI recipients.

Other Rules: VSI recipients must agree to serve in the reserves. If they leave the reserves for any reason other than medical disabilities, their annual payments end.

Reservists who later qualify for military retired pay will have the full amount of their VSI payments deducted from their retirement checks. VSI recipients who later qualify for VA disability compensation will lose $1 of VSI money for every dollar of VA money they receive.

DISABILITY SEVERANCE PAY

Every year, people leave the military because they're unable to meet the rigid physical requirements of active-duty service, although their medical problems are relatively minor and they're expected to be able to have productive careers in the private sector.

Disability Severance Pay Summary:	
Purpose:	Financial transition aid for injured veterans
Formula:	Lump-sum, based on Basic Pay, years of service
Amounts:	Vary widely
Taxable:	Generally, yes. Not for combat-related
Loopholes:	Health problems don't have to originate with on-base, on-duty activities
Problem Areas:	Payback for VA disability, not retirees.

For them, the services provide Disability Severance Pay—also known as Medical Severance Pay—which helps ease the transition back to civilian life.

Eligibility: Disability Severance Pay is given to people on active duty with medical problems that prevent their continued service in uniform.

A formal Physical Evaluation Board must select a person for Disability Severance Pay. Four major groups don't receive Disability Severance Pay:

• Those with less than six months in the military (including reserve time calculated at the rate of one day per "point").

• People whose disabilities were caused by situations while incarcerated, absent without leave, or through "willful misconduct."

• Those with at least 20 years on active duty. (They're eligible for regular length-of-service retirements.)

• Servicemembers with disabilities officially rated as being at least 30 percent. (They can qualify for a more generous military disability retirement.)

Rates: Disability Severance Pay is a one-time, lump-sum payment given to qualified servicemembers, usually on their last day on active duty.

A simple two-step formula—with some unexpected fine print—is used to calculate the amount of Disability Severance Pay.

1. Multiply the person's monthly Basic Pay by 2.

2. Take that figure and multiply it by the number of years in the military.

Military members whose disabilities are discovered during pre-promotion physical examinations are eligible to use the Basic Pay for the rank they would have held if they'd been promoted.

Note that the rate formula is based upon time in the military, not just active-duty time. Reservists and National Guardsmen receive one day's credit per "point" under this formula.

Periods of six months or more are rounded to the higher year. Periods less than six years are rounded to the lower year.

Taxes: The general rule on Disability Severance Pay is that it's taxable. Certain narrowly defined groups of people can receive tax-free payments.

Eligible for tax-free payments are people whose Disability Severance Pay was based on health problems caused by the following:

- Armed conflict.
- Hazardous service.
- "Conditions simulating war," such as maneuvers or training.
- "An instrumentality of war," such as weapons or terrorism.

Other Rules: Recipients of Disability Severance Pay who later qualify for VA disability compensation will lose $1 of VA money for every dollar of Disability Severance Pay they received.

People who receive Disability Severance Pay aren't considered military retirees. Their connection with the military is ended when they leave active duty. They are ineligible for care in military hospitals or other on-base service.

EIGHTEEN

RETIRED AND DISABILITY PAYS

In This Chapter:
- *Typical Military Retired Pay*
- *Reserve Retired Pay*
- *Fifteen-Year Retired Pay*
- *Temporary Disability Retirements*
- *Military Disability Retirements*
- *VA Disability Compensation*

People who devote a large portion of their working lives to the military are entitled to lifelong benefits from the government, including monthly pensions, certain medical benefits, and access to on-base resources such as commissaries and exchanges.

Also entitled to lifelong financial help from the government are the men and women whose health has been permanently harmed by their military service. For them, the Department of Veterans Affairs (VA) operates a program called disability compensation.

TYPICAL MILITARY RETIRED PAY

Twenty years of honorable service on active duty justifies military retired pay for the rest of one's life. That has been the basic principle underlying the military's system for retired pay for decades.

Retired Military Pay Summary:	
Purpose:	Pension, deferred pay
Amounts:	Varies widely
Formula:	By date joined military
Taxable:	Yes
Loophole:	Combine with VA disability
Problem Areas:	Divorce; federal civil service

The retirement program for military professionals is technically known as "nondisability retirement," to distinguish it from the military's disability retirement program, which is discussed later in this chapter. Also following later is the retirement program for reservists, which is fundamentally different from the one for active-duty military personnel.

Three Retirement Systems: Military people are covered by the retirement system that was in effect when they first joined the military, not the one in effect when they retire. There are three retirement systems for people now in uniform.

Basic Plan: Covering people who joined the military before September 8, 1980, recipients of the Basic Plan are eligible for 2.5 percent of the last monthly amount of Basic Pay for each year of service, to a maximum of 75 percent of Basic Pay at 30 years. There is a full annual increase in cost-of-living adjustment.

High-Three Plan: This plan covers people who joined the military between September 8, 1980, and July 31, 1986. The retirement formula is based on average monthly Basic Pay for highest three years—or, more properly, 36 months—on active duty. Recipients are eligible for 2.5 percent of the "High-Three" average for each year of service, to a maximum of 75 percent of "High-Three" average Basic Pay. There is a full annual increase in cost-of-living adjustment.

Redux Plan: This plan covers people who joined the military after July 31, 1986. The retirement formula is based on average monthly Basic Pay for highest three years—or more properly, 36 months—on active duty. Rates start at 40 percent of "High-Three" average at 20 years, increasing by 3.5 percentage points for each following year, to a maximum of 75 percent of "High-Three" average at 30 years.

For Redux Plan retirees, COLA increases will be set at one percentage point less each year than inflation, as measured by the Consumer Price Index. At 62, retired pay will be recalculated. It will be reset at the monthly amount that Redux retirees would have had if they'd received full COLA increases since their retirements. Thereafter, once again, their COLA increases will lag inflation by one percentage point.

Rates: For the people who retire in 1996, here's how much retired pay they'd receive monthly during their first year out of uniform, looking at only three years-of-service marks:

	20 Years	25 Years	30 Years
O-10	$4,508	$5,635	$6,762
O-9	4,053	5,379	6,515
O-8	3,841	4.919	5,902
O-7	3,472	4,341	5,209
O-6	2,659	3,636	4,577
O-5	2,406	3,112	3,735
O-4	2,082	2,602	3,122

O-3	1,806	2,250	2,700
O-2	1,336	1,670	2,004
O-1	1,054	1,317	1,581
OE-3	1,827	2,284	2,741
OE-2	1,547	1.933	2,320
OE-1	1,309	1,636	1,963
W-5	1,924	2,568	3,112
W-4	1,728	2,302	2,888
W-3	1,521	1,969	2,446
W-2	1,364	1,774	2,128
W-1	1,266	1,583	1,899
E-9	1,462	1,998	2,533
E-8	1,281	1,771	2,261
E-7	1,130	1,583	2,035
E-6	990	1,237	1,485
E-5	840	1,050	1,261
E-4	677	846	1,010
E-3	581	726	870
E-2	490	612	735
E-1	437	546	655

The second major grouping—OE-1, OE-2, and OE-3—covers officers with previous experience as enlisted members or warrant officers.

Tax: The normal 20-year military retirement is fully taxable for federal and state income taxes. Some tax protections are available to retirees with military disability retirements, as discussed later in this chapter.

Divorce: Federal law permits state divorce judges to award a portion of a military retiree's pension to an ex-spouse as part of a divorce settlement. Once these settlements have been approved by a judge, a military finance center can send that money directly to the ex-spouse: It doesn't go to the retiree.

Federal Employment: Some military retirees who have second careers may lose some of their pensions. These rules affect only a small number of retirees.

Regular Officers: Those with military commissions that are technically Regular can keep their full civil service salaries, plus about the first $9,000 yearly in military retired pay and half the amount of retired pay in excess of $9,000. The $9,000 figure rises annually. This provision doesn't affect former enlisted members or reserve officers, including those who retired from active duty.

$108,000-Plus Incomes: Military retirees working as federal civil servants cannot have their combined retired pay and civil service salary exceed Level V of civil service's executive pay scale. Everyone at that level loses however much retired pay is necessary to stay below the mark.

RESERVE RETIRED PAY

When people make a commitment to the government by staying active in the reserves and the National Guard, the government responds by making a commitment to them. If they spend a total of 20 years in the military—in any mixture of active duty, Guard, and reserve time—the military will offer them retired pay.

Reserve Retired Pay Summary:	
Purpose:	Pension, deferred pay
Formula:	Date entered military defines system
Amounts:	Vary widely by rank, years of service, "points"
Taxable:	Yes
Loopholes:	Combine with VA disability
Problem Areas:	No payment until age 60; "good" years; divorce; federal civil service.

Although the reserve retirement system has some broad similarities with the active-duty retirement system, it's not as generous. Twenty years in the reserves won't yield the same retired pay as 20 years on active duty.

Eligibility: Reservists and National Guardsmen must accumulate 20 years' service that are officially rated as "good" or "creditable." A "good" or "creditable" year is one in which a reservist accumulates at least 50 "points."

Reservists and Guardsmen receive one point for each day on active duty, for each drill period (meaning, they get four points for a typical weekend drill), and for certain blocks of instruction.

For reservists and Guardsmen, military retired pay begins on the 60th birthday.

Rates: Reservists are governed by the three different retirement systems discussed above. Entry into the reserves or the active-duty force is the key factor for determining which retirement system affects a particular individual.

Determining a specific reservist's retired pay is a four-step process.

1. Add up the number of points earned throughout the reservist's military career, both active duty and in the reserves.

2. Divided that number by 360 to convert points into years.

3. Multiply the number reached in step 3 (the point-equivalent of years) by 2.5 percent.

4. Multiply that figure by the Basic Pay for the reservist's rank and years of service. Use the pay chart in effect when the reservist begins drawing retired pay.

This is the way the amount of retired pay is determined for people under the Basic Plan for military retirement. Appropriate changes must be made in step 4 to reflect provisions of the High-Three Plan and the Redux Plan.

COLAs: Like their active-duty counterparts, retired reservists

and retired National Guardsmen have periodic—usually annual—increases in their retired pay known as Cost-of-Living
Adjustments (COLAs).

Also like their active-duty peers, reservists and Guardsmen covered by the Redux Plan for military retirement will see
their COLAs fixed at one percentage point less than inflation
each year.

Federal Employment: With one narrow exception, the
decision of retired reservists and retired Guardsmen to work as
federal civil servants has no effect on either their military retired pay or their civil service salaries.

That exception involves people whose combined retired pay
and civil service salaries exceed the $108,000-plus figure of
Level V of the federal civil service's executive pay scale. More
details are in the "Federal Employment" section under "Typical
Military Retired Pay" above.

FIFTEEN-YEAR RETIRED PAY

A relatively new program allows some military people to retire
after spending less than 20 years in uniform. These early
retirements are a management tool used by authorities in
reducing the size of the military.

Fifteen-Year Retired Pay Summary:	
Purpose:	Drawdown tool
Amount:	Varies widely
Formula:	By rank, years of service, early-retirement penalty
Taxable:	Yes
Problem Areas:	New program with misunderstandings.

Commonly called the 15-year retirement, the program is officially known as the "Temporary Early Retirement Authority," or TERA, program. In this case, "temporary" refers to the military's authority to approve these early retirements.

Eligibility: Military officials select people with between 15 and 20 years on active duty for early retirement. Recipients must agree to accept the early retirements.

Rates: All participants fall into one of the three basic retirement systems discussed above. The entry date into the reserves or the active-duty force determines the formula used to calculate an individual's retired pay.

A three-step process is used to calculate a 15-year pension:

1. Multiply the number of years the servicemember has spent on active duty by 2.5 percent.

2. Subtract from the number derived in step 1 one percentage point for each year less than 20 years.

3. With the number produced by step 2, multiply the servicemember's last amount of monthly Basic Pay.

The result is the service member's monthly retired pay.

This is the way the amount of retired pay is determined for people under the Basic Plan for military retirement. Appropriate changes must be made in step 1 to reflect provisions of the High-Three Plan or the Redux Plan.

COLAs: Like the more typical 20-year military retirees and retired reservists, most 15-year retirees have periodic— usually annual—increases in their retired pay known as Cost-of-Living Adjustments, or COLAs.

Also like their 20-year and reserve peers, 15-year retirees covered by the Redux Plan for military retirement will see their COLAs fixed at one percentage point less than inflation each year.

Other Benefits: Recipients of 15-year retirements are entitled to the same retired benefits as 20-year and reserve retirees, including medical care and lifelong access to on-base facilities, such as commissaries and exchanges. Folks with more traditional military retirements don't get anything denied to 15-year retirees.

Reservists: A 15-year retirement is being offered to members of the reserves and National Guard. Rates are computed by adapting the reserve retirement formula to the basic features of the 15-year retirement. That includes a penalty of one percentage point for every year less than 20 "good" years before retirement.

TEMPORARY DISABILITY RETIREMENTS

Sometimes when military people encounter serious medical problems, they can find their careers in limbo. Doctors aren't sure the person is sick enough to be discharged, although they're clearly not well enough to go to work.

Temporary Disability Retirement Pay Summary:	
Purpose:	Pay while medical problem is evaluated
Formula:	50 to 75 percent of Basic Pay
Amounts:	Monthly, $404 (E-1 at 50%) to $3,502 (0–5 at 75%)
Loophole:	No duties for recipients
Problem Areas:	Five-year duration; can end sooner.

When a military person's fitness for active duty is in question, the services have the option of putting that person on the Temporary Disability Retirement List (TDRL) until the situation clears up. People receiving money under this program are said to be "on the TDRL."

Eligibility: Technically, the TDRL is open to active-duty people who are unable to perform their military jobs because of a medical problem. Those health problems may not be permanently disabling, or if permanent, the degree of the disability must be uncertain.

Physical Evaluation Boards examine the records of military personnel and decide who is placed on the TDRL. Military personnel have a right to present their case to their boards. They can argue to go on the TDRL, to be discharged, or to return to active duty.

People on the TDRL are officially considered military retirees. They have no official duties. They are ineligible to live on base. They lose eligibility for any military payments except TDRL money.

TDRL cannot be combined with VA disability compensation. TDRL retirees who accept VA money are discharged.

Rates: Two formulas are used to compute pay for TDRL people. Those folks can choose the most generous formula:

• Multiply their last monthly Basic Pay by the percentage of disability assigned to them by a Physical Evaluation Board.

• Multiply their last monthly Basic Pay by 12. Multiply that figure by 2.5 percent for each year on active duty. Take that number and divide by 12, yielding a monthly rate.

Whatever formula is used, personnel on the TDRL are guaranteed a minimum of 50 percent of their Basic Pay, but they cannot receive more than 75 percent of Basic Pay.

Although some of the special pays related to hazardous duty (see chapter 7, "Hazardous Duty Pays") have provisions allowing payment for hospitalized personnel, folks on the TDRL are ineligible because they're retired.

Duration: As soon as the medical condition of those on the TDRL stabilizes, they are reevaluated. Then they are either returned to active duty or discharged.

People discharged with lingering medical problems are either given Disability Severance Pay (see chapter 17, "Discharge

Pays"), military disability retirements, or VA disability compensation. The last two programs are discussed in this chapter. The longest anyone can stay on the TDRL is five years. If a person's medical condition is still uncertain at that time, he or she is discharged.

Time spent on the TDRL counts toward promotions and time in service for pay purposes, but it doesn't count toward regular length-of-service retirements.

MILITARY DISABILITY RETIREMENTS

The military is a dangerous place to spend a working life. Even in times of peace, the quietest military base is filled with such things as explosives, large equipment and people acting under stress and fatigue, and people traveling to exotic regions of the world—all factors that increase the risk of accidents and illness.

Military Disability Pay Summary:	
Purpose:	Pay for service-related disabilities
Formulas:	By disability percentage or years of service
Amount:	Varies dramatically
Taxable:	Varies
Loophole:	Combined with VA disability compensation
Problem Areas:	Fixed level of disability; access to military hospitals.

A small number of injured and ill veterans find that their needs are best met by receiving Military Disability Pay. It's classified as a retired pay, and recipients are considered military retirees.

Eligibility: All military members—active duty and reservists—can receive disability retirements from the armed forces if they are unable to perform their official duties because of a health problem.

The disability must be permanent, based upon standard medical practices. It must be caused by a person's military service or aggravated by military service.

To qualify, people must have disabilities that are rated as being at least 30 percent. Generally, recipients must have at least eight years on active duty. People with less time in uniform can qualify if they can show that the disability wasn't caused by misconduct.

Rates: In most instances, there are two formulas that can be used to compute the size of a veteran's military disability retired pay. The servicemember gets the more generous formula.

• Multiply the servicemember's monthly Basic Pay by the percentage of the disability.

• Multiply the servicemember's monthly Basic Pay by 2.5 percent for each year on active duty.

In this calculation, the figure for Basic Pay is the Basic Pay for the last month on active duty for those who first joined the military before September 8, 1980. For those who joined more recently, the figure for Basic Pay that's used in the equation is the monthly average for the 36 months of highest pay.

Special Circumstances: Here's how the rules for military disability retirements affect certain kinds of people, along with some other details about the program.

Applications: Veterans can apply for a military disability retirement at any time, even years after they've left active duty.

Changes: The disability percentage assigned to a recipient of military disability retired pay never changes, even if the medical condition deteriorates. If a disability worsens, the military expects servicemembers to seek VA disability compensation, discussed below.

Other Benefits: Recipients of military disability retired pay are military retirees, just like their length-of-service counterparts. They are eligible for commissary and exchange privileges and carry military ID cards. They can be treated in military medical facilities, although they're subject to the same access problems as other military retirees.

Retirees: People who already qualify for regular length-of-service retirements because they have at least 20 years on active duty can have part of their retired pay consist of disability retired pay. That amount is the same percentage as the disability.

Tax: The general rule on military disability retired pay is that it's taxed. There are three specific exceptions. The following groups *don't* have to pay taxes on their disability retirements:

• People drawing military disability retired pay on September 24, 1975, or at an earlier date.

• People who had joined the military by September 24, 1975, and who later qualified for military disability retired pay.

• Veterans whose military disability retirements were based upon combat injuries.

In these cases, tax protection extends to the military disability retired pay. Other income, including military retired pay *not* based upon a disability, is subject to taxation.

VA: Recipients of military disability retired pay must give up $1 of that money for each dollar they receive in VA Disability Compensation, which is discussed below. As a practical matter, most disabled military retirees discover they can receive more from the VA system than from the military's.

VA DISABILITY COMPENSATION

Most veterans receiving money from the government for service-related medical problems actually receive their checks not from the Defense Department, but from the Department of Veterans Affairs (VA).

VA Disability Compensation Summary:	
Purpose:	Pay for service-connected medical problems
Formula:	By degree of disability
Amounts:	$91 monthly to $1,870 (1996)
Taxable:	No
Loophole:	Increases if condition deteriorates
Problem Areas:	Linkage with military service; military retired pay.

These payments are called VA Disability Compensation. Recipients aren't classified as military retirees unless they qualify for one of the military retirement programs discussed above.

Eligibility: Disability compensation can be paid to anyone who served in the military, including members of the reserves and National Guard. There is no minimum time that a person must spend in uniform to qualify.

Two major groups of veterans are *ineligible:*

• Veterans with discharges officially rated as "under dishonorable conditions."

• Veterans with disabilities caused by "willful misconduct," such as those incurred during commission of a crime, during unauthorized absences, or through the abuse of drugs or alcohol.

The disability can be the result of an accident, injury, or illness. It could have arisen during military service or it could have been aggravated by military service.

To be eligible, a veteran must prove a link—usually through military medical records—between the disability and military service. Recipients don't have to prove that the medical problem was caused by official duties.

Rates: VA Disability Compensation is a monthly payment. Amounts are expressed as a percentage. Those percentages, in turn, are based upon medical evaluations of the severity of a veteran's impairment.

For 1996, here are the monthly rates in effect, based upon the percentage of disability:

Disability	Amount
10 %	$91
20	174
30	266
40	380
50	542
60	683
70	862
80	999
90	1,124
100	1,870

The amount of money assigned to each percentage usually changes every year to keep pace with inflation. The disability percentage can change if a veteran's medical problems worsen or improve.

Other Benefits: The monthly check for VA Disability Compensation isn't the most important benefit that many recipients get. They also receive free, lifelong medical care in VA hospitals and clinics for their disabilities.

Here, a crucial distinction arises. People with disabilities rated 40 percent or lower can be treated only for the disability.

People with disabilities rated at 50 percent or higher can be treated for anything in a VA hospital or clinic.

Also available to veterans with VA Disability Compensation are a range of other programs, including vocational training, dependents allowance, and dependents' health care.

Military Retirees: The VA's Disability Compensation can be paid to military retirees. That includes people who qualify for the military's regular length-of-service retirements and military disability retired pay.

For each dollar of VA money, a military retiree must give up $1 of DoD money.

NINETEEN

SPOUSES, EX-SPOUSES, AND SURVIVORS

People wearing uniforms aren't the only ones who have a stake in the military compensation system. Spouses, ex-spouses, survivors, and even the children of active-duty people and reservists have some rights regarding a military paycheck.

In this chapter, we'll explore some of the financial programs and financial rights of the family members of military personnel. This is more of a summary than a comprehensive listing.

Anyone—spouse, ex-spouse, survivor, or guardian—who is making important financial decisions should get face-to-face help and the latest information from a military lawyer, family support center, or other on-base experts.

SPOUSES

Time was when military personnel were overwhelmingly male and spouses were female. The wife stayed home to take care of the kids. The military man took care of earning money to pay the family's bills. And that was that.

Of course, that picture of the typical military family changed decades ago. But that view still shapes many of the regulations and federal laws affecting the rights of spouses and other family members to the pay of an active-duty military member or a reservist.

Military Paycheck: Active-duty military personnel can designate a spouse or a child to receive monthly direct payments from a finance center. Those payments, deducted from the military member's monthly pay, are called allotments.

All of the services have regulations that require military members to help their families financially. An array of pressures can be brought upon folks who don't live up to family responsibilities, starting with counseling by chaplains and unit commanders, Article 15s and Captain's Masts, even courts-martial and discharges.

Note that several types of military pay, especially the housing allowances—BAQ, OHA, and VHA—have separate rates for people with dependents and people without dependents.

An active-duty member claiming those payments at the with-dependents rate when the dependents aren't being financially supported is receiving that extra money fraudulently. That's a serious charge. And the military will take it quite seriously.

Missing: When military members become prisoners of war, missing in action, or are put "on missing status," they continue receiving their regular pay and allowances.

They can earn promotions, accrue leave, and get the benefit of pay raises. Any allotments to spouses that were in effect before they were declared missing continue.

Mental Incompetence: When military members become mentally unable to manage their own affairs, family members may need formal court orders designating them as guardians or trustees to gain access to the member's full military pay. Until a court-appointed guardian has been named, the Army and Air Force designate The Adjutant General as the trustee of the military member's pay. The Navy and Marine Corps name the finance center as the trustee.

EX-SPOUSES

In the military, it's often not easy to separate personal concerns from professional ones. Perhaps for that reason, the military offers some protections after a divorce to the former spouses of active-duty personnel.

What follows here is a summary of some of those protections. This isn't all that you need to know if you're facing the difficult decisions involved in a divorce. This is a review that will help you learn the right questions to ask as you gather more comprehensive, up-to-date information.

Military Paycheck: When the military receives a court order involving financial support for a servicemember's divorced spouse or children, the military can send a part of an active-duty person's pay directly to an ex-spouse or dependent children.

The military doesn't need a servicemember's permission. It can act if the servicemember is two months' behind in alimony or child support.

Servicemembers are supposed to be notified before any action is taken by the finance center on such a claim. Unless the servicemember can show that the payments were made already or the court order is erroneous, the finance center is going to honor the court order.

The finance center can send the following to the ex-spouse:

• Up to 50 percent of the servicemember's "disposable income" if the servicemember has remarried or supports a dependent child.

• Up to 60 percent of the servicemember's "disposable income" if the servicemember hasn't remarried and hasn't acquired a dependent child.

• An additional penalty of 5 percent of the servicemember's "disposable income" if the active-duty person is at least 12 weeks behind in those payments.

What's "disposable income?" Generally, it's everything that goes into a military paycheck *except* the following:

• Basic Allowance for Quarters.
• Basic Allowance for Subsistence.
• Clothing allowances.
• Family Separation Allowance.
• Overseas Cost-of-Living Allowance.
• Overseas Housing Allowance.
• Travel allowances.
• Uniform allowances.

Also not included in "disposable income" are regular deductions for the following:

• Debts to U.S. government.
• Federal income tax.
• Servicemen's Group Life Insurance premiums.
• Social Security tax.
• State income tax.
• Survivor Benefit Plan premiums.
• Debts and fines to federal government.
• Contributions to the Armed Forces Retirement Home.

Moving: When servicemembers and their spouses break up during a stateside assignment, the military has no obligations to help the spouse and dependent children move out of the military member's home.

When the breakup is overseas, the government will help. Basically, the military will treat the move of the civilian spouse and dependent children back to the states as a PCS move. (For more, see chapter 15, "Moving Payments.")

Those moves must be completed within a year of the divorce or annulment, or within six months after the servicemember is reassigned from the overseas station, whichever comes first.

Two pieces of fine print are important. First, the spouse and children must be officially "command-sponsored." Second, the couple must be overseas when a divorce becomes effective or on the date of annulment.

Retirees: If a military retiree fails to abide by a court order for alimony or child support (note: this doesn't include property settlements) the ex-spouse can send the finance center a copy of the court order and request a direct payment.

For money owed an ex-spouse as a property settlement, there are some preconditions before a military finance center will make direct payments to the ex-spouse. The marriage must have lasted at least 10 years, and at least 10 years of the marriage must have been spent on active duty.

Other government-paid benefits are due to three specific groups of ex-spouses:

• *Free medical care for one year:* Married at least 20 years, to a military member who spent at least 20 years on active duty, at least 15 years of the marriage on active-duty. Divorce completed after April 1, 1985.

• *Free medical care for life:* Married at least 20 years, to a military member who spent at least 20 years on active duty, at least 15 years of the marriage on active duty. Divorce completed before April 1, 1985.

• *Free medical care for life, plus commissary and exchange access:* Married at least 20 years, to a military member who spent at least 20 years on active duty, at least 20 years of the marriage on active duty.

After receiving a proper court order, finance centers can send money owed to a retiree directly to the ex-spouse. Usually, the most that a finance center can send is 50 percent of a retiree's "disposable income." That figure can rise to 65 percent when delinquent child support and alimony are included.

"Disposable income" includes retired pay the retiree declines to accept or waives to receive VA disability compensation (See chapter 18, "Retired and Disability Pays"). It does *not* include premiums paid for the Survivor Benefit Plan, or federal and state income taxes.

SURVIVORS

When people die on active duty, the financial bedrock provided by the government to the spouses and children is Dependency and Indemnity Compensation (DIC). It will provide them with a regular monthly income.

DIC Summary:	
Purpose:	Income for families after deaths on active duty or from related causes
Amounts:	$810 monthly (1996)
Formula:	None, one flat rate
Loophole:	Extra payments for children; rate higher for earlier deaths
Problem Areas:	Proving link between service and death.

DIC payments are also made to the family members of reservists who die in the line of duty. It also goes to survivors of veterans who die after their discharges, but from service-related causes.

Eligibility: Separate eligibility rules affect the service-member and any survivors seeking DIC.

The military member must have died on active duty, active

duty for training, or inactive-duty for training ("drill" periods), or after discharge from health problems caused or aggravated by military service.

Note that people who die on active duty, even from off-base causes unrelated to military service, meet the first eligibility requirement.

Eligibility rules for post-discharge deaths are complex. Since the primary readership of *Military Money Guide* comes from the active-duty ranks, it's sufficient for them to know that DIC is a program that touches people long after leaving the military.

So far as survivors are concerned, separate eligibility rules apply to spouses and children. To qualify, spouses must have been married for at least one year, if childless or for any duration with children, living continuously with the servicemember since marriage (except for separations through no fault of spouse), and not be remarried.

If there is no surviving spouse, or if the spouse is ineligible for DIC, the children of servicemembers and veterans can qualify for DIC in their own right. To be eligible, children must fall into one of these categories:

• Not yet 18.

• Not yet 23 and a full-time student in approved course of study.

• Older than 18 and incapable of self-support because of physical or mental disability that began before the 18th birthday.

Military people who have more than 20 years on active-duty and who are still on active duty at the times of their deaths have their spouses protected financially by the Survivor Benefit Plan (SBP), discussed below.

Rates: Spouses who qualify for DIC receive the same monthly payment. In 1996, it was $810 per month. Generally, the rate increases annually to keep up with inflation.

Spouses of servicemembers and veterans who died before

January 1, 1993, are covered by a different rate structure that is based upon the rank of the military person.

The spouse's monthly DIC can be increased by several factors. Here are those factors, plus the monthly 1996 rates for those conditions:

- For each child younger than 18—$205.
- Surviving spouse housebound—$99.
- Surviving spouse blind, or in nursing home or in need of home-care—$205.

When there is no surviving spouse or when the surviving spouse is ineligible for DIC, the following monthly rates in 1996 were paid to eligible children of the servicemember:

- One child—$344.
- Two children—$496.
- Three children—$643.
- Each additional child after third—$126.

Those monthly payments to eligible children can be increased under certain situations:

- Disabled child over 18 (no DIC spouse)—$205.
- Disabled child over 18 (spouse gets DIC)—$344.
- Child 18 to 23 and in school—$174.

DIC rates are unaffected by other sources of income or Social Security payments. Nor does a DIC payment affect Social Security payments.

Reservists: Survivors of reservists and National Guardsmen seeking DIC must establish a link between their servicemember's death and health problems caused or aggravated by military duty.

SURVIVORS OF RETIREES

When military people retire, they're eligible to collect retired pay for the rest of their lives. But retired paychecks stop after the death of a veteran.

> ### SBP Summary:
>
> | | |
> |---|---|
> | Purpose: | Income for survivors of retirees |
> | Amounts: | Vary greatly |
> | Formula: | Percentage of retired pay |
> | Taxable: | Yes |
> | Loophole: | No cost for active-duty personnel |
> | Problem Areas: | Retiree pays premiums; one-time sign up; limited rules for canceling. |

The Survivor Benefit Plan (SBP) is a government-backed program to ensure that the wives and husbands of deceased military retirees will have an income if they are left alone.

Eligibility: Separate rules affect the servicemember and the survivors seeking SBP payments.

The servicemember must be retired from active duty, still be on active duty with at least 20 years, or be a reservist with 20 "good" years.

So far as survivors are concerned, separate eligibility rules apply to spouses and children. To qualify, spouses must have been married for at least one year if childless, or have been married for any duration with children.

Spouses who remarry before their 55th birthdays lose eligibility for SBP payments. Eligibility is restored if those new marriages end. Spouses who remarry after their 55th birthdays can continue receiving SBP payments.

The children of eligible veterans can qualify for SBP coverage. They can be protected along with their surviving parent, or they can be covered separately. To be eligible, children must fall into one of these categories:

• Not yet 18.

• Not yet 22 and a full-time student in approved course of study.

- Older than 18 and incapable of self-support because of physical or mental disability that began before the 18th birthday.

Rates: How much a survivor receives under SBP is determined by the amount of the military retiree's retired pay and by certain decisions the retiree makes.

The most that a survivor can receive is 55 percent of the servicemember's retired pay (or, in the case of people who die on active duty with at least 20 years' service, 55 percent of Basic Pay).

Retirees can choose lesser amounts of coverage. Spouses of retirement-eligible people on active duty are automatically given the maximum coverage.

The first step in calculating SBP coverage comes when the retirees selects a "base," a portion of retired pay. Whatever the base, the survivor will get 55 percent of it.

Reserve retirees have three decisions after they accumulate 20 "good" years:

- They can put off a SBP decision until they begin receiving retired pay at age 60.

- They can decide to provide immediate SBP benefits for survivors in the event of death.

- They can decide that, in the event of death, SBP payments will begin for survivors on what would have been the retiree's 60th birthday.

SBP coverage is free only for active-duty people with at least 20 years. Active-duty retirees usually have 6.5 percent of their "base" withheld from retired pay as a premium.

Reserve retirees don't pay any premiums until they begin receiving retired pay at age 60. As with active-duty folks, the normal cost is 6.5 percent of the "base." For reserve retirees electing earlier coverage, they pay for the extra, early service in the form of slightly higher premiums once they begin collecting retired pay.

All survivors will experience a drop in SBP payments on their 62nd birthdays, when they begin receiving Social Security. Basically, SBP reduces by the amount of Social Security, meaning there's no overall drop in income.

For retirees and spouses who don't want this reduction in SBP payments, supplemental insurance is available from the military that provides extra protection for extra premiums.

INDEX